JEREMY RAISON

Jeremy Raison is a writer and director working across film, television and theatre. He was Artistic Director of the Glasgow Citizens Theatre for seven years during which time the company nearly tripled its box office, was nominated for seventy three awards and toured work to Singapore, Hong Kong, South Africa, Germany and the USA, as well as the West End. He also ran Chester Gateway Theatre for four years for which he won the TMA/Stage Award for Outstanding Achievement in Regional Theatre.

Other awards and nominations include the Marrakech Film Festival Gold Star, Manchester Evening News Best Touring Production, Liverpool Post and Echo Best Production, BBC Radio 4 Young Playwrights Award, Plays and Players Best Children's Play Award, Real to Reel Best International Short Film and a CATS Award for Best Production for Children and Young People.

He is the author of more than 30 plays including The Rain Gathering (National Theatre, Traverse, Radio 4), The Sound of My Voice (Citizens, Assembly), Blitz (Traverse), Charlie and the Chocolate Factory (Sadlers Wells, national touring), Don Juan (Citizens), Heart and Soul (Chester Gateway), Wake Me In the Morning (Oran Mor), Jumping Jack Flash (Liverpool Everyman), Savage Britannia (National Theatre Studio, Mandela), A Distant Shore (National Theatre Studio) and A Child of Europe (Theatre Workshop) and plays for BBC Radio 3 and 4 and Amazon Audible.

ALSO BY JEREMY RAISON

Wake Me In the Morning
The Rain Gathering
Candyland
Bring Me Sunshine
The Sound of My Voice adapted from Ron Butlin
Heart and Soul a play with live music

Therese Raquin

by

Jeremy Raison

adapted from the novel
by Emile Zola

I3 PUBLISHING

First published by 13 Publishing in Great Britain, 2014

ISBN 978-1-909809-07-9

A CIP catalogue record for this book is available from the British Library

Cover photograph © Richard Campbell

For information on the author: www.jeremyraison.com

This stage version of *Therese Raquin* was first performed at the Glasgow Citizens Theatre on 17 September 2004. The cast was as follows:

THERESE	Carla Henry
CAMILLE	Daniel Weyman
LAURENT	Dermot Kerrigan
DOCTOR	Kevin McMonagle
MADAME RAQUIN	Anne Lacey

CHORUS Drew Taylor, Jessica Williams and Lynne MacLachlan

All other parts were played by members of the company.

Director	Jeremy Raison
Designer	Soutra Gilmour
Lighting Designer	Charles Balfour
Composer	Corin Buckeridge
Choreographer	Ethelinda Lashley-Johnstone
Fight advisor	Carter Ferguson

CHARACTERS

THÉRÈSE
CAMILLE
LAURENT
MADAME RAQUIN
DOCTOR

A NOTE ON PRODUCTION

The original production was designed as a piece of physical theatre with a minimal set. A chorus was used to suggest the menace and claustrophobia of Paris. The chorus can be as large or small as required.

ACT ONE

1.
Black

A black front cloth. We bleed through to see...

...a boat being pulled by a boy along a stretch of water.

Two street kids start to play hopscotch in the water, splashing....

An older couple take a short cut through this dirty arcade in Paris, he with too many parcels, she leading the way...

Suddenly the street kids run round them, between them, and with a final mighty splash, run off.

A confident man (Laurent) passes **a dainty woman** (Thérèse), notices her and then knocks her **slight male companion** (Camille), so the latter stumbles towards the water...

a slow moment...

until the man just manages to pull himself back upright and they continue on their way.

Dripping pipes - steam coming out of the sewers – streets in mist – a never ending black roughly plastered wall – an arcade seen through a dirty glass roof. The whole place feels like an underground gallery, lit only by three funeral lights. The Avenue Pont Neuf, as we see projected:

Thérèse Raquin

Long shadows slide over the flags. A man appears.

Another projection:

A Love Story.

A woman, clutching a bag to her, hurries past - scurrying to leave this horrible place, this cut-throat's alley - without stopping, a hint of steel as she passes the man, runs up a staircase to escape.

And the man follows her.

Another passer by, a blind tramp has appeared. The blind tramp starts to wave his cane, begins to wave it faster and faster until it is a solid sheet of white – on this white glimmering wall of cane can be read projected:

Love Can Be Murder

A group/chorus appear through a waterfall of rain. They huddle under umbrellas.

….a 21 year old **Thérèse** is revealed from the shadows of this group – pushing her way out, trying to escape, finally moving away…

Just for a moment, film noir bars of light cross her face, her eyes and then…

She's in the shop: cobwebs and dusty discoloured material…

A sign says 'Haberdashery' in big letters on a long narrow plank above the doorway. And on the window can be made out, written in red, 'Thérèse Raquin'.

…**Madame Raquin**, a pale fleshy woman aged about 53, is also disgorged from the group. A man whispers to her, and she heads for the shop, back from an errand.

MME RAQUIN: Did you hear about the murder last night? In the Rue de l'Ecole de Medecin. Terrible: a poor young woman.

Thérèse sits in profile, unspeaking.

MME RAQUIN: They say she must have known her attacker. But of course no one knows anything. You'll need to be careful. A murderer walking the streets, it makes me shudder just thinking about it.

Suddenly a cat screeches. Madame Raquin jumps.

MME RAQUIN: Oh! Those terrible cats!

Thérèse hasn't so much as flickered.

MME RAQUIN: You're not ill, are you, Thérèse? How you can sit so still is beyond me. I thought marriage would bring you out of yourself…

She trails off into silence, still talking but her voice unheard.

Inside the shop, a clock ticks increasingly loudly. The boring hours. Nothing happens.

Madame Raquin is still talking, incessant, exhausting.

Finally the clock strikes ten o'clock. Madame Raquin sighs deeply.

MME RAQUIN: Well, another good day for us, we must thank the Almighty.

She nods, self satisfied. Thérèse doesn't move.

MME RAQUIN: Are you coming up? Well, I'll see you in just a minute, don't be long.

Madame Raquin turns out all the lights except one and goes out, leaving the door open.

Shopkeepers lock up for the night: various calls of 'bonsoir', as…

Thérèse is left alone, isolated in dim light.

Only the jewellery shopkeeper opposite still watches.

At last Thérèse begins to move. She has the tired, stiff movements of an old woman as she goes to close the door Madame Raquin left open.

She turns back to the shop and begins to weep. Sobs, then, surprisingly, unexpectedly, huge gulps, a great wash of grief

As fog sweeps in and the shop sweeps out…

2.
The fog becomes morning mist over the river, five years before.

Thérèse is taken back to the past: the lush verdant fields of Vernon, Monet country. It's bright. A Sunday. The sound of water. They're beside the river. A dark outer layer of clothing is peeled off, she lets loose her hair, she is 16 years old. Low on the ground, lithe, coiled, full of unseen power, she sways with her hand in the river.

Sickly, spoilt 20 year old **Camille**, and his 48 year old mother arrive. He's tired.

MME RAQUIN: Thérèse, what are you doing?
THÉRÈSE: Just cooling myself –
MME RAQUIN: No playing on Sunday, please.

Thérèse stops as Madame Raquin sits. Camille puts his head in his mother's lap. Madame Raquin strokes his hair. It's very hot

For a moment, peace and quiet. Water and the sound of birds and crickets.

CAMILLE: We've walked a long way, haven't we?
MME RAQUIN: (almost a lullaby) My poor boy –
CAMILLE: Maman, your knees are digging into me.

Madame Raquin shifts. She's uncomfortable now, but Camille is happy. He drifts off to sleep.

THÉRÈSE: I love the water, the way it glides wherever it wants -
MME RAQUIN: Shh, Camille's trying to sleep –
THÉRÈSE: Can't we walk further, see where the river takes us, Aunt?

MME RAQUIN: Thérèse, please.

Thérèse is frustrated. She already speaks in a whisper, moves without a sound. But she's hot and sticky, trails her arm lazily in the water, throws water at -

MME RAQUIN: Stop that, you'll splash him!

Madame Raquin has jerked and woken Camille, who is suddenly coughing.

MME RAQUIN: Oh for goodness' sake, now look what you've done, child. Pass me my bag. Hurry, Thérèse!

Thérèse gets the bag quickly, hands it to Madame Raquin. Madame Raquin pulls out Camille's sickly looking sea green medicine. She feeds him with it:

MME RAQUIN: My poor fragile darling – here.

Camille's coughing is getting worse, but he fends off Madame Raquin's spoonful of medicine.

MME RAQUIN: Thérèse, help me!

Finally Thérèse holds Camille. He responds to her better than his mother.

Madame Raquin is brutal – cruel to be kind: she holds his nose and pours the medicine down him. Camille splutters, but finally he is calm.

MME RAQUIN: Perhaps we came too far.
THÉRÈSE: (under her breath) If you'd just stop fussing over him –

MME RAQUIN: Thérèse, he's not well! I take care of you willingly but Camille's health –
THÉRÈSE: Takes precedence.
MME RAQUIN: We do both love Camille, don't we, child? We know his needs. (To Camille) There, there, my darling, that's better now, isn't it?

Camille is calmer, Madame Raquin strokes his damp hair. Silence for a moment, until:

THÉRÈSE: Tell me about my father.
MME RAQUIN: There's nothing to tell.
THÉRÈSE: Please -
MME RAQUIN: Really, there's nothing.
THÉRÈSE: Why did he go to Africa?
MME RAQUIN: Because he was a fool!

She won't say more.

THÉRÈSE: Did you ever meet my mother?
MME RAQUIN: Camille, are you rested enough to walk home yet? It'll be dark before we know it.
THÉRÈSE: I thought we were going on -
MME RAQUIN: We've come quite far enough. You've both done very well, haven't you?
CAMILLE: Yes, maman.

Thérèse wants to ask more questions but says nothing.

MME RAQUIN: Isn't this bliss? Far better than trudging on for no reason whatsoever. (To Thérèse) You should take your medicine too –
THÉRÈSE: It's not for me –
MME RAQUIN: Thérèse, don't be obstinate, it does you a

world of good. Don't give me one of your looks.
THÉRÈSE: I didn't -

Madame Raquin stares at her. Their eyes lock. Then Thérèse tilts her head down.

MME RAQUIN: What's good enough for my darling is good enough for you.

Thérèse acquiesces: the medicine goes down. Thérèse almost gags on the spoon.

MME RAQUIN: One more. Good. Every little helps. (already tidying up) Come, darling Camille. Thérèse, time to go home.

As Madame Raquin gathers her bag and sunshade, Thérèse spits out the medicine behind her back. Camille sees, but says nothing.

Madame Raquin takes Camille by the arm. He pulls his arm away.

CAMILLE: I'm not an invalid!
MME RAQUIN: (ignoring him) Thérèse, my bag, if you please.

Madame Raquin takes tight hold on Camille again and they head off. Behind them, Thérèse reluctantly picks up Madame Raquin's bag, and follows.

As they leave, Thérèse hurls the bag at the back wall, where it explodes – a riot of colour dripping down the back wall.

3.

Immediately the lights change – the water's gone - and Thérèse (17) is alone, outside, at home. It's early evening.

THÉRÈSE: (singing) Sur le pont D'Avignon
On y danse on y danse
Sur le Pont D'Avignon
On y danse
Tout en rond

Camille comes to join her. Despite his age (21), he behaves like a child with Thérèse.

CAMILLE: There you are! Maman wants you inside.
THÉRÈSE: On a beautiful day like this!
CAMILLE: Y-you should be more grateful.
THÉRÈSE: Why?

Camille doesn't say: because she took you in. He's a bit frightened of her.

CAMILLE: Just go.

Thérèse still doesn't move.

CAMILLE: She needs help, stupid!
THÉRÈSE: Then why don't you?

Thérèse stares at him, a challenge.

CAMILLE: W-when we're married, you won't speak to me like this.
THÉRÈSE: You don't need a wife, you need a nursemaid!
CAMILLE: I'm n-not ill! I just need fresh air and exercise.

THÉRÈSE: Then tell her – go on, be brave. Refuse your medicine.
CAMILLE: Fight me.
THÉRÈSE: Be a man for once –
CAMILLE: I know, a wrestling match!

Thérèse gives up.

THÉRÈSE: Your mother needs me.
CAMILLE: Let's run down to the water. I'm fed up being stuck inside. Let's run until we collapse –
THÉRÈSE: Or drown.
CAMILLE: Let's go somewhere completely new!

For a moment Camille shows a bit of passion. Thérèse stares at him. Camille can't work out what she thinks.

THÉRÈSE: You really think you can fight me?

Camille is standing very close to Thérèse. Suddenly she pins him to the ground, lies on him. Their faces are very close together. She notices, but he doesn't seem to realise: the position is sexual. He just stares at her blankly, more like a petulant boy:

CAMILLE: Get off me, Thérèse. That hurts.

Thérèse gets off him. As she does so, he attacks her, lashing out with his feet to trip her. Taken off guard, she finds him on top of her.

CAMILLE: The winner! You lose, Thérèse!

He stands up first and then casually dribbles spit down onto her face.

Thérèse leaps up like a wild animal, blazing with anger. This is a side of her Camille has never seen before.

Thérèse throws herself on Camille, both fists raised. Battering him, crashing blows into him, overwhelming him, knocking him to the ground, kicking him ferociously as he lies there.

CAMILLE: Thérèse, stop! Get off me! Ow! Thérèse, no!!

Camille, shocked, tries to slide away from her across the ground, terrified, utterly subdued. Finally he curls into a foetal position. She kicks him one last time. He's crying.

THÉRÈSE: Who's the winner now?

She wipes the spit off her face.

CAMILLE: Thérèse?
MME RAQUIN: (off) Thérèse!

Simultaneously Madame Raquin has called from some way away (the house).

Thérèse doesn't move, slightly shocked at her own strength, pumped up like a proud boxer.

4.
Days pass. Weeks pass. Years pass.

Thérèse stands, her impressive youthful strength gradually hidden as time passes.

Camille rises up and circles Thérèse, increasingly wary of her. Thérèse gets older before our eyes. Less of a girl, more of a repressed woman. She ties her hair up tightly as Camille circles. She tidies her clothes, buttons herself up tightly.

Leaves fall, life swirls around Thérèse as a table, chairs appear.

5.
Madame Raquin bustles on. It's five years later, the same year as the play's opening – Camille is now 25, Thérèse 21, Madame Raquin 53.

MME RAQUIN: Come in here, please, children. I wish to speak with you.

She leads them to the table.

CAMILLE: This sounds exciting. Or worrying, eh, Thérèse?

Camille keeps his distance from Thérèse, sits down before she does.

CAMILLE: What's Thérèse done now?
MME RAQUIN: Thankfully, she's done nothing.
CAMILLE: That's a first.
MME RAQUIN: Camille, settle down.
CAMILLE: You're being mysterious, maman.

Thérèse says nothing. They wait. Madame Raquin is nervous but determined.

MME RAQUIN: It's time we discussed both your futures.
CAMILLE: What future?
THÉRÈSE: We're fine as we are.
MME RAQUIN: Your future together.

Thérèse looks startled, reacts by almost exploding/falling off her chair, unseen by the other two – like a split personality, her inner feelings revealed

MME RAQUIN: Thérèse is old enough now to be married.

Thérèse's inner self is horrified: she twists and turns, desperate to escape her fate.

CAMILLE: Married? Really?
MME RAQUIN: Thérèse?

Suddenly Thérèse snaps back into her chair, hiding her real feelings, smiling.

MME RAQUIN: I hope it's no surprise. To either of you, I've harboured such... hopes for a long time.

The inner Thérèse grieves her lost life, watching from a distance as the conversation continues round the table.

MME RAQUIN: It's really the ideal solution. The only one. Thérèse can take care of you, Camille. And you can look after her. It's a perfect match.

Camille doesn't know what to say.

CAMILLE: Yes, maman.
MME RAQUIN: Good boy. Thérèse?

Camille looks towards Thérèse's chair, as does Madame Raquin. Once again, Thérèse snaps back into the chair, unmoving, hiding her real feelings.

MME RAQUIN: Thérèse? What do you think? The decision concerns you as well.

Thérèse doesn't reply. It's awkward.

MME RAQUIN: Camille -
CAMILLE: Yes?
MME RAQUIN: I think you should go and study.
CAMILLE: Yes, maman.

Camille watches from the distance. Thérèse grieves in her chair.

MME RAQUIN: You see, Thérèse, it kills two birds with one stone. You know each other, you love each other. This way you no longer have to worry about the future, do you? When my brother brought you to me you were an unexpected - addition… A gift from God, of course. You were sent for a reason, but nevertheless –

Thérèse watches Madame Raquin in perfect silence, unmoving. It's unnerving.

MME RAQUIN: Thérèse, my brother was - he was a good man. When he arrived here, with you, swaddled - out of the blue! - you had no one! All the way from Algeria!

Thérèse's movements show her desperation.

MME RAQUIN: I believe I have always done my best by

you. You would have died a pauper. You could never have survived!

Thérèse still doesn't react.

MME RAQUIN: Oran. That's where you were born. Your mother - was a native woman - your father said – said she was the most beautiful…creature he had ever seen. She was a savage!

As Madame Raquin talks, the chorus start dressing Thérèse for her wedding.

MME RAQUIN: How could he marry her? Impossible. How could he possibly leave you in that ungodly country? He did the right thing, bringing you to me!

Thérèse is still frighteningly calm. It unnerves Madame Raquin.

MME RAQUIN: He - was going to come back, he planned to, of course but. But then he left and I - Killed by one of those dreadful diseases in that terrible country, may God have mercy on his soul.
THÉRÈSE: And my mother?
MME RAQUIN: I pray for her too. I'm all you have. And Camille.

Finally Thérèse is dressed. A sacrificial lamb to the slaughter.

MME RAQUIN: You'll be happy.

The veil comes down over Thérèse's face.

6.

Camille appears, dressed for his wedding. Madame Raquin joins their hands together.

CAMILLE/THÉRÈSE: Pour nous aimer fidelement
Dans le bonheur ou dans les epreuves
Et nous soutenir l'un l'autre
Tout au long de notre vie

Camille and Thérèse are bound together as rose petals are thrown over them.

7.

The light changes. The wedding night - Camille leads Thérèse into the bedroom.

CAMILLE: See, Thérèse, it wasn't so difficult was it? You - you just turn right at the top of the stairs instead of left.

As they enter the room the smell of disinfectant almost makes Thérèse sick. There are roses all round the wedding bed.

THÉRÈSE: Sorry, I feel –
CAMILLE: We've drunk too much!
THÉRÈSE: I didn't drink –
CAMILLE: Thérèse, my wife!

He makes a grab for her.

THÉRÈSE: Wash first.
CAMILLE: Wash?

THÉRÈSE: I want to remember our first night with pleasure.
CAMILLE: Wash -

Camille staggers to the washing bowl – he dips his face right in. For a moment, he looks like a drowned man. Turns to see Thérèse, she's nervous. So is he. He strips off his shirt.

CAMILLE: Scrub my back, please?

Camille gives her a sponge. He bends over.

THÉRÈSE: But it's covered in –

She forces herself to wash his pimpled back. Camille takes great pleasure from it. Thérèse is revolted.

CAMILLE: Harder, Thérèse, scrub harder like maman.

He turns to kiss her, she sidesteps him.

CAMILLE: Come to bed, Thérèse -
THÉRÈSE: Wait - I need to wash.
CAMILLE: After –
THÉRÈSE: I'm dirty. And tired. It's been a long day.
CAMILLE: And what a long night it'll be.
THÉRÈSE: You **are** drunk -

He looks as if he's about to be sick.

CAMILLE: Come to bed.

Thérèse stalling for time, washing obsessively. Camille watches, moves to fondle her. She pushes him off.

THÉRÈSE: In a minute!

Camille starts to cough.

THÉRÈSE: Go to bed. Keep yourself warm, dear Camille.

Camille gets into bed. Thérèse can stall no longer. Her look of dread, unseen by Camille.

Thérèse goes towards the bed. She climbs in. Camille moves over to her. She shudders. Camille climbs on top of her, tries to undo her clothes –

THÉRÈSE: What are you doing?
CAMILLE: You're my wife!
THÉRÈSE: You'll tear it -

Thérèse pushes Camille off. Then undoes her garments. Again Camille climbs on top of her. He's rough.

THÉRÈSE: Ow! Camille, that hurts.
CAMILLE: It's your wedding night, it's meant to hurt -

And then Camille starts to cough, on top of her, convulsively.

THÉRÈSE: Camille –
CAMILLE: (reaching for a bottle) I need my medicine.
THÉRÈSE: Leave it!

Camille is bewildered. She sees his look, and then lies back down. Camille climbs on top of her again.

THÉRÈSE: Camille, be gentle.
CAMILLE: You're my wife.

THÉRÈSE: Let me help you.
CAMILLE: You're my wife.
THÉRÈSE: No, Camille, no, that's not right –
CAMILLE: (angry and frustrated at his own ineptitude) You're my wife!

She puts her hand down to stop him, and suddenly he has ejaculated prematurely.

CAMILLE: Oh!
THÉRÈSE: Oh -

Thérèse can't hide her revulsion - and then relief.

THÉRÈSE: Poor Camille -
CAMILLE: I'm no one's poor anything!

Camille tumbles off, embarrassed, turns away from her. Thérèse looks at him for a moment, then gets up, heads for the washbowl. She starts to wipe her stained undergarments off with a sponge. She is impassive. Behind her, Camille is silent.

A screeching cat can be heard in the distance.

Thérèse stands, facing the great black wall, leprous with scars. She looks out at the blackness.

Finally Thérèse climbs back into bed. It's cold. She can't sleep.

8.
Madame Raquin appears and listens for noises upstairs. She hears only the screeching cat. She sits and listens with her

knitting, but gradually falls asleep.

The light comes up, it is morning. Madame Raquin wakes rather stiffly. Upstairs everything is silent. She goes to lay the breakfast table: a fancy breakfast for the newly weds.

Camille comes in, unkempt, in a dressing gown. As Thérèse dresses upstairs, the following conversation happens downstairs:

MME RAQUIN: And how's love's young dream this morning? My boy - My Man! Oh, let me take a good look at you -

She wraps the dressing gown round him, to keep him warm. He shrugs her off.

MME RAQUIN: Weddings are exhausting. Your father and I -
CAMILLE: Maman, please!

Madame Raquin doesn't quite know what to say next.

CAMILLE: Thérèse and I talked.
MME RAQUIN: And will continue to do so, for the rest of your lives.
CAMILLE: And we-we're – we're…
MME RAQUIN: Yes, Camille?
CAMILLE: We're leaving Vernon!
MME RAQUIN: You'd like a picnic?
CAMILLE: No, you don't understand. We – we're leaving f-for ever!
MME RAQUIN: I don't follow.
CAMILLE: And moving to Paris.

MME RAQUIN: Camille, think: you're not well enough for city life. No.

CAMILLE: Maman, you're not listening to me!

MME RAQUIN: We're happy, why spoil this? And how would we afford it? Be sensible.

CAMILLE: I'll work!

MME RAQUIN: It's such an expensive city, they rob you blind soon as look at you -

CAMILLE: Y-you can't wrap me up forever in c-cotton wool!

MME RAQUIN: Darling, don't let Thérèse tell you what to do, you're the man of the house now.

CAMILLE: And it's decided!

MME RAQUIN: And I refuse! Absolutely.

Camille doesn't know what to say.

CAMILLE: (calm) Maman, I have always done as you said. I m-married my cousin for you. I took all the m-medicines you gave me -

MME RAQUIN: Of course you take them –

CAMILLE: Finally when I j-just w want something, for myself –

MME RAQUIN: Camille -

CAMILLE: The least you can do is agree with me!!

An impasse. Silence.

MME RAQUIN: See sense, please, child –

CAMILLE: I'm not a child!

MME RAQUIN: Come, sit down, have some breakfast, marriage is always unsettling at first -

CAMILLE: I shall m-make myself ill!

MME RAQUIN: No, you won't!

CAMILLE: I shall hurt myself!
MME RAQUIN: Camille, stop this!
CAMILLE: I'll K-KILL MYSELF!!

Madame Raquin is at a complete loss, when Thérèse arrives in the room, fully dressed.

MME RAQUIN: Thérèse, please, do something with your husband. He has some ridiculous notion about moving to Paris.

Thérèse says nothing. They both look at her.

MME RAQUIN: Thérèse?

A pause, then Thérèse finally breaks the silence:

THÉRÈSE: It is decided.

Madame Raquin doesn't know what to say. For a moment, Thérèse and Camille could almost be complicit.

Suddenly the house explodes – a storm arrives - rain, thunder. As Paris appears…

9.
Boxes, packing cases, a riotous mess. Appearing like tumbleweed, brought by the chorus.

In Paris it's drizzling – gloomy, wet, damp. Fetid. There's stuff everywhere, they've not yet unpacked their furniture from Vernon, their table and chairs…

The trio are seen with cases arriving in this new place.

Madame Raquin arrives in their new home first. Surveys it. She seems unsure. Is just turning up the dull gaslight when Camille arrives:

CAMILLE: You said this was a good area!
MME RAQUIN: And we're going to be happy here, aren't we? The old lady who sold it had no idea what a bargain it was –
CAMILLE: The arcade full of people, lovely window displays, fine rooms -
MME RAQUIN: And we'll make it like that, won't we? A touch of paint here and –
CAMILLE: This isn't what I wanted!

Madame Raquin is terrified of another tantrum.

MME RAQUIN: Camille, when the sun's out, it won't feel so dark. You'll see. A good sweep and whitewash and this place will be home in no time.

Camille doesn't seem impressed. It looks as if he wants to stamp his feet like a child.

Thérèse arrives. Immediately Camille changes tack.

CAMILLE: It's fine. We'll only be up here in the evenings. I'll be at work all day: a good job in a large firm, that's what I'm after.
MME RAQUIN: Then that's what you shall get, won't he, Thérèse? My clever little Camille.
CAMILLE: Shiny cuffs and a pencil behind my ear, I'll be so busy I won't be back from work til late. You'll have each other. And the shop.

Thérèse is devastated. Giving up the sunshine of Vernon for this. Even if she can't show her dismay.

MME RAQUIN: Oh my dear, we are going to be happy here, aren't we? We'll hang new curtains, new wallpaper! We'll put flowers in the windows – lay new carpets. Thérèse, come and help me put these things away.
THÉRÈSE: No.

Madame Raquin stops in the face of Thérèse's implacable passivity.

THÉRÈSE: We're fine as we are.

Slowly Madame Raquin starts to tidy the mess of the move on her own.

Outside the flat, chorus members scurry home like rats, their footsteps irritating.

10.
The **Doctor** comes into the flat from a bedroom with an enema syringe, which he puts away in his doctor's bag. He's a cheery soul, roughly the same age as Madame Raquin. Behind them, Thérèse leaves the flat with a chamber pot.

DOCTOR: Bed rest and warm blankets, that's what he needs, yes? The Paris damp doesn't agree with the poor boy. Mind you, can't say it agrees with many of us. You'd have to be insane to live here! But we all do!

The Doctor chuckles merrily.

MME RAQUIN: How much do I owe you?
DOCTOR: Nothing. For an old friend.
MME RAQUIN: But I must pay something –
DOCTOR: Nonsense, it's a pleasure to see you again, Madame Raquin. Who'd have thought, eh? That you'd call me out. Of all the doctors in this great city. Delightful. And what a charming wife your son has.

Thérèse is just passing back to Camille's bedroom at this moment.

MME RAQUIN: He's always suffered. The times I've nursed him –
DOCTOR: I remember well.
MME RAQUIN: You've no idea how much strain it put me under - At death's door from the moment he was born -
DOCTOR: It would worry any mother.
MME RAQUIN: Even if it brought us closer.
DOCTOR: Absolutely. Well, he'll survive again, madame, I can assure you.
MME RAQUIN: Thank you.
DOCTOR: Nonsense, I did nothing. Absolutely nothing.

He laughs merrily again.

DOCTOR: Well. I suppose I have other patients waiting - on est toujours occupe!

He starts to go with a shrug.

MME RAQUIN: Doctor, would you accept the honour of dining with us?
DOCTOR: No, really. I couldn't! My word.
MME RAQUIN: It's the least we can do.

DOCTOR: Well, then, perhaps – yes! Why don't we all say yes more often?

The Doctor is about to settle down at the table when she says:

MME RAQUIN: It's settled then. Next Thursday?
DOCTOR: Oh. Yes. Next week. Of course. Indeed, next Thursday I believe I might be - Good day.

The Doctor takes his hat and disappears, as Thérèse comes in from Camille's bedroom. Madame Raquin is about to head off to see Camille when Thérèse stops her.

THÉRÈSE: He's trying to sleep.

Madame Raquin heads for the table and her cash-box instead.

MME RAQUIN: To think they only asked twelve hundred a year rent. It's a steal. I can buy stock for the shop and pay the first year's rent without eating into my capital. See, Thérèse? In subsequent years, the shop's profits and Camille's salary – when he gets a job - will be more than enough for our needs.
THÉRÈSE: I could work too.
MME RAQUIN: No, Thérèse. You're lucky. Your place is at my side.

Thérèse is trapped.

11.
The light changes – a new day, as Camille appears:

CAMILLE: They've offered it to me!

MME RAQUIN: Oh, darling Camille, how wonderful!

CAMILLE: Junior clerk in the offices of the Orleans Railway Company!

MME RAQUIN: Isn't your husband clever, Thérèse?

CAMILLE: It'll be slow progress, of course. There's lots of other bright sparks there already. Brighter than me, no doubt.

MME RAQUIN: You missed a great deal of school -

CAMILLE: But it suits me. I'll work my way up, you'll see.

THÉRÈSE: (under her breath) Pen pusher.

MME RAQUIN: Pardon?

CAMILLE: No, Thérèse is right, isn't she? That's what I'll be. A pen pusher! And I'm delighted. It's what I've always wanted! To be a humble cog in some glorious machine!

He continues to talk – time passes. It's clear there's no escape for Thérèse…

12.

…as the Doctor joins them for a game of dominoes.

CAMILLE: They're asking me to work harder. With no rise in salary. But only until my promotion. But I'm not unhappy where I am. At least I'm not responsible when there's a rail disaster like last week's. Our department may be called the Office of Works, but we only shuffle papers. It's the men on the ground who're to blame!

The Doctor yawns surreptitiously.

MME RAQUIN: All the same it was terrible for you,

wasn't it, darling?
DOCTOR: Three disasters in as many years, yes?
CAMILLE: Accidents happen.

Thérèse, apart now, looks as if she could hang herself.

MME RAQUIN: Thérèse, are you joining us, my dear?
THÉRÈSE: Play without me –
MME RAQUIN: It's better with four.
THÉRÈSE: I don't feel well.
MME RAQUIN: The doctor's here –
DOCTOR: Leave her.
CAMILLE: Perhaps if Thérèse took her medicine?

They turn away from her, Madame Raquin giving her attention to the Doctor.

Thérèse can barely breathe in this stuffy atmosphere. She feels buried alive, watching mechanical corpses, which nod their heads and move their arms and legs about whenever their strings are pulled.

The eerie silence – just the clicking of dominoes – and yellowish light exaggerates the domino players' ugly faces. The image fills Thérèse with terror. Her hands feel feverish, a pricking sensation. She tries to hide it.

But finally flees.

The Doctor finishes a set of dominoes with a firm clack.

MME RAQUIN: I'll see where she's got to.
CAMILLE: No, let me.

Camille goes out after her.

13.
Camille brings Thérèse back in, like a prisoner. Time has passed: Thérèse is now 24, Camille 28, Madame Raquin 56.

CAMILLE: I found this strange little creature hiding downstairs in the dark.
THÉRÈSE: I went to lock up.
DOCTOR: I hope it's not me. (he laughs) I can't believe I've been coming here three years today!
MME RAQUIN: Is it really?
DOCTOR: Must be some sort of world record, yes? Every Thursday like clockwork!
MME RAQUIN: People will talk.
DOCTOR: Or think Camille really very ill indeed!

The Doctor laughs heartily. Madame Raquin laughs along.

MME RAQUIN: Very good, Doctor, yes, very good.
DOCTOR: How's your promotion coming along, Camille?
MME RAQUIN: Oh, you know how it is, Doctor: seniority, nepotism, old school friends.
CAMILLE: Have you read Buffon?
DOCTOR: You've been reading Buffon?
CAMILLE: I'm studying him.
DOCTOR: Fantastic stuff.
CAMILLE: And the History of the Consulate and Empire by Thiers.
MME RAQUIN: Camille's serious about improving himself. Thérèse won't read at all.

The Doctor is getting up to go. They are all tired.

34

DOCTOR: Well -
MME RAQUIN: One more game, Doctor!
DOCTOR: You're keeping me from my bed!

He seems in good humour, but Madame Raquin isn't quite sure. Once he is gone, Madame Raquin starts to tidy up. Until Camille pipes up:

CAMILLE: Oh, I nearly forgot, maman, someone's coming tomorrow after work –
MME RAQUIN: Who?
CAMILLE: Oh, I can't tell you.
MME RAQUIN: Do you know, Thérèse?
CAMILLE: Don't try to guess, you'll only spoil the surprise.

14.
As the Doctor leaves, the friend arrives.

This new man is roughly the same age as Camille (26) but everything that Camille is not – charismatic, strong, at ease with himself, handsome, with large strong hands and an imposing presence: **Laurent**. Camille holds him, proprietorial.

CAMILLE: Recognise this gentleman?

Madame Raquin looks at the stranger but has no idea. Thérèse is watchful.

CAMILLE: You don't know Laurent? Son of old Laurent. Who had those cornfields near Jeufosse? You really don't remember? You must! He fetched me every morning for school, you gave him bread and jam -

MME RAQUIN: Of course! But you've grown.

CAMILLE: I should hope so!

MME RAQUIN: It must be…oh, twenty years or more! Oh, and those boots. I'll never forget your huge farmer's boots. If it hadn't been for me, you'd never have had decent shoes for school, would you?

CAMILLE: Maman, don't embarrass him –

MME RAQUIN: Who'd have thought? That little boy turning into such a fine man.

CAMILLE: He's been working in the same office as me for the last eighteen months! And we only realised yesterday! That's how big the company is - and of course Laurent's doing well, much better than me! He's a real high-flyer, already on fifteen hundred a year! His father sent him to college to study law. And he's learned to paint! He's an artist!

LAURENT: Well, hardly –

MME RAQUIN: Laurent, of course you'll dine with us.

LAURENT: I wouldn't want to impose –

MME RAQUIN: It would be an honour. We so rarely see people from Vernon.

LAURENT: Then I accept!

MME RAQUIN: That's settled then. What about next week?

LAURENT: So what are we having?

Laurent puts down his hat on the table, practiced and at ease. He smiles at them all.

Madame Raquin is a tiny bit put out, but has no choice.

Thérèse watches, transfixed. She studies Laurent's strong hands, which he keeps spread out on his knees. He has a lazy confidence. A little shiver runs through her as she looks at his bull neck.

CAMILLE: You remember my wife, don't you, Laurent? Cousin Thérèse? She's changed quite a bit!
LAURENT: (a moment's hesitation) Of course. I recognised Madame Raquin straight away.

Laurent looks her straight in the eye. Thérèse feels herself pierced to the core. A slow moment suspended in time… Laurent takes her hand and bows low.

THÉRÈSE: Any friend of my husband's is a friend of mine.
LAURENT: Likewise.

…and back to normal speed as Camille interrupts.

MME RAQUIN: How's your father?
LAURENT: No idea. We've fallen out. Haven't spoken in – oh, five, maybe six years.
CAMILLE: You're joking!
LAURENT: The old man is impossible. His latest is taking the neighbours to court. I often wondered if that wasn't the real reason he packed me off to law school!
CAMILLE: You didn't want to be a lawyer?
LAURENT: I pretended to attend lectures for my twelve hundred franc allowance. Spent every penny, didn't do a stroke of work. Shared digs with another student – a painter. Now that's living! So I painted too. We used to smoke and play cards all day long –

The Raquin family can't quite believe him.

LAURENT: Sadly, the old fool caught me red-handed. Too

good to last, anyway. Cut me off, told me to get back to the farm or he'd disown me. So - I painted religious subjects, to get rich quick to be honest, but – ach, it didn't work, no money in it! Wasn't long before I was down to my last sou, saw myself dying of starvation!

The bell rings. Madame Raquin looks to Thérèse to answer it, but Thérèse doesn't move.

LAURENT: Had to find a job. Ended up working for the same corporate monster as poor Camille here.
CAMILLE: (delighted) Yes, it is a monster, isn't it!

The bell downstairs rings again.

MME RAQUIN: (not altogether willingly) I'll just see who it is.
LAURENT: (as soon as she's gone) Bastard'll die one day, just have to put off the painting career 'til then.
CAMILLE: But t-that's terrible –
LAURENT: Why? Christ, I'm mediocre.
CAMILLE: That's not true -
LAURENT: You'd know, would you?

Camille has no answer.

LAURENT: You know the only thing I really miss?
CAMILLE: What?
LAURENT: The studio. Well, the women. The never ending supply of nudes. That's the trouble with working for the railway. And the canteen food's a disgrace.
CAMILLE: The women don't really take their clothes off?
LAURENT: Of course.
CAMILLE: In front of you?

LAURENT: Where else?

CAMILLE: Isn't that a bit - ? I - I'd be embarrassed. I mean - no, seriously.

Laurent stares at his own great, spread out hands. He may not show it, but he is very aware of Thérèse. Watching.

LAURENT: I had one model. A beautiful red-head, she had the most amazing delicate white skin. Stunning breasts also and – (he leans towards Camille) and an extraordinarily soft navel, which fluttered gently under my fingertips as I slipped my fingers down into -

Laurent stops as Madame Raquin returns. He looks up and sees Thérèse watching his last voluptuous gesture, her gaze fixed, her mouth half-open, licking her dry lips.

Thérèse stops as soon as she sees him watching her. Laurent looks from Thérèse to Camille, and holds back a smile.

MME RAQUIN: No one there.

LAURENT: (to Camille) I should paint you.

CAMILLE: Me?

LAURENT: It's summer, we're out of the office at four, I could come round here for a couple of hours every night.

THÉRÈSE: No!

They all look at Thérèse.

MME RAQUIN: Thérèse?

THÉRÈSE: I'm sorry, I was…day dreaming.

LAURENT: If it's too difficult -

MME RAQUIN: Nonsense! Thérèse is just being silly. We're too used to our own company.

CAMILLE: Yes, you have to come and paint me. I insist!
MME RAQUIN: And you can stay for dinner every evening.
CAMILLE: I'll curl my hair, and put on my best jacket.
LAURENT: I'll polish you off in a week.

15.
Simultaneously the bedroom appears. An easel, with a box of paints. Camille is puffed up, posed uncomfortably with a pipe. Laurent lazes on the marital bed, studying him, occasionally getting up to add dashes of paint to the canvas.

LAURENT: This is the life! A good dinner, grand company and a paintbrush! God, the stories I could tell you. There's nothing better than a mistress…

Just at this moment, Thérèse enters. Laurent looks at her briefly then turns away.

LAURENT: …and a bottle of wine - I should paint Thérèse as well. Your wife has the most extraordinary bone structure. There's a superb specimen hidden under those clothes. Oh, Camille, I mean purely in anatomical terms.
CAMILLE: No offence –
LAURENT: Well, please speak up if I say anything I shouldn't.

Camille has moved and Laurent has to reposition him.

CAMILLE: I'm not worried by anything you say. And she's a blank! She doesn't have a thought in her head.
LAURENT: Is that so, Thérèse?

Laurent stares at Thérèse. Who calmly, quietly, surprisingly holds her own.

Slow: the mystery of attraction.

Then back up to speed.

LAURENT: I believe you!

Laurent laughs, Camille joins in. Laurent is very aware of Thérèse watching him paint.

LAURENT: Certainly beats being a minor clerk in the railways! They're imbeciles! I could sort out the railways in ten minutes flat if they'd let me!
CAMILLE: Well, you're cleverer than me –
LAURENT: But what's the use? I tried; when I first started. But no one listens. Now I just keep my head down. You know, I think I've finished. Christ, what'll I do with my evenings now? It's not often you find yourself in such devastating company. (turning to Thérèse) Like it?

Thérèse doesn't comment.

LAURENT: Where did you find such a perfect wife? I should paint you next, Thérèse, a blank canvas is always the best.
CAMILLE: You have an open invitation to come back any time.
LAURENT: There!
CAMILLE: Really? You're finished! Can I see it? No, I must fetch maman. And champagne. Champagne and maman. Don't move, I'll be right back!!

And Camille is gone. Leaving Thérèse and Laurent alone.

LAURENT: Would you like me to bring you to life, Thérèse? I can always use a model.

Laurent picks up the painting, moves close to her.

LAURENT: What do you really think of the painting? Not much, is it? But then he's really not much of a subject.

Laurent offers Thérèse the paintbrush.

LAURENT: Want to deliver the last brushstroke? With love for a doting husband? Tell me, Thérèse – Why on earth would someone like you marry him?

Thérèse acts shocked by the question. He reaches out to her, and she shies away before he can touch her, like a highly strung race-horse. Then suddenly:

LAURENT: You're not happy.
THÉRÈSE: What sort of question is that?
LAURENT: It's not a question. Camille? For Christ's sake?!
THÉRÈSE: I won't have you talking about my husband like that!
LAURENT: You expect him to die soon?
THÉRÈSE: Stop this!
LAURENT: Then I don't understand -
THÉRÈSE: Why should you? You, with your models –
LAURENT: Are you jealous?
THÉRÈSE: How dare you!
LAURENT: You've been watching me – every single moment I've been here.

Laurent is moving towards her now, predatory, dangerous – they still haven't touched.

LAURENT: Every moment I've been here, your eyes boring into the back of my neck, Thérèse, don't pretend –
THÉRÈSE: Don't flatter yourself!
LAURENT: Don't you ever dream? Desire? Don't you want anything for yourself?
THÉRÈSE: Escape!

A moment as Thérèse realises what she has said.

THÉRÈSE: I didn't mean that. I didn't say it.
LAURENT: You can't take it back now –
THÉRÈSE: I do! I do take it back.
LAURENT: Your marriage is a joke, isn't it?
THÉRÈSE: That's not what I meant!
LAURENT: Yes you did, look at him!
THÉRÈSE: It wasn't my fault!

Laurent attempts to kiss her roughly. She pushes him off, slaps him hard. He looks startled. He's not used to failure.

Suddenly she attacks him – slaps him, grabs his hair, smothers him with kisses. And then they're pulling each other down, she sits astride him and he fucks her, lying on the floor – quickly.

Laurent hears footsteps coming up the stairs - panics – tries to pull away – she holds him down.

LAURENT: Thérèse, off!

She won't move.

LAURENT: Now!

He manages to pull away from her, scurries away to the other side of the room to dress. She's left on the floor. More noise outside.

LAURENT: (whispered) Thérèse, come on - Get up! Christ, they're coming.

Camille and Madame Raquin appear: Laurent looks terrified. Thérèse gets up, casual.Camille has champagne.

CAMILLE: I had to go out for it – maman had none in the house - two bottles! – Let's celebrate!
MME RAQUIN: Thérèse, what are you doing on the floor?
THÉRÈSE: I tripped. Laurent must have left something lying around.

Madame Raquin has handed Laurent champagne. His hand shakes.

MME RAQUIN: (to Laurent) Our artist is nervous.
LAURENT: I don't like showing my work. In case you don't like it. I'm keen you think well of me. All of you.

Laurent passes champagne to Thérèse. The others can't see the look they give each other.

CAMILLE: (childishly delighted) It's wonderful. Maman, come and look!
MME RAQUIN: Quite so. Darling Camille, it's you! (running out of things to say) What do you make of it,

Thérèse? You've been watching our maestro closely.

THÉRÈSE: The eyes are too close together. And he's green.

MME RAQUIN: Thérèse, there's no need to be rude -

THÉRÈSE: It doesn't even look like Camille. It's vile!

MME RAQUIN: Thérèse, apologize!

LAURENT: Madame Raquin, everyone's entitled to an opinion.

MME RAQUIN: Well, I like it. I really do. I think it will look splendid hung in this very room.

THÉRÈSE: Our bedroom?

CAMILLE: (delighted) Oh, Maman!

MME RAQUIN: Thérèse is wrong. Laurent, it's a triumph. A masterpiece!

Thérèse picks up a loose paintbrush, takes it to Laurent while Camille and his mother study the portrait.

THÉRÈSE: (quick, whispered, but self assured) There's a backdoor from the alley, tomorrow afternoon, two o'clock…

Laurent senses they're being watched.

LAURENT: Thank you, Thérèse.

MME RAQUIN: I hope that was an apology.

CAMILLE: More champagne?

THÉRÈSE: I told Laurent to clear up his mess next time.

LAURENT: Until the next time.

THÉRÈSE: You've not had enough of us now the painting's complete?

MME RAQUIN: Thérèse, please! It's a wonderful painting, Laurent. Thank you. You've made Camille immortal.

16.

Thérèse undresses, slowly, languorously – she ends up in her camisole and petticoat.

THÉRÈSE: If you only knew how much I suffered In that horrible room. Sleeping every night with Camille until I was thirteen! The smell made me sick! He refused to take his medicines unless I shared them…

She starts to weep. She's talking to Laurent, who's there, holding her in his arms.

THÉRÈSE: The nights I spent in that bedroom. With Camille coughing and groaning. Hawking his spit. I had to squat in front of the fire, endlessly watching his medicines boil. My Aunt scolding me whenever I moved. I only wanted to be outdoors, pine trees swaying, water rippling, the wind breezing through my limbs; I used to dream of running barefoot along dusty roads, begging, living the life of a gypsy! But I could barely walk. They hobbled me. I couldn't run! I who should have been carried on my mother's back through deserts. Instead they brought me here!

LAURENT: We must end this.

THÉRÈSE: Don't tell me you're not happy, not now -

LAURENT: What if she comes up?

THÉRÈSE: She won't.

LAURENT: Thérèse, please, be sensible –

THÉRÈSE: Oh, easy for you, isn't it? Free food, free drink, and me waiting like one of your whores!

LAURENT: You despise me!

THÉRÈSE: No, I – I -

LAURENT: What?

THÉRÈSE: (She can't say she loves him, instead angry) You won't believe how vicious they made me! Turning me into a hypocrite and a liar! I don't know if there's blood left in my veins! When you first saw me, I was a dumb animal, wasn't I? I used to bite my pillow at night to stifle my screams, I could have thrown myself in the Seine.

She kisses Laurent on the neck.

Suddenly Camille is there – he doesn't see Laurent - they are in different times. She is in bed with Laurent while speaking with Camille.

CAMILLE: But, Thérèse. You're my wife.

THÉRÈSE: I'm tired, Camille, please –

CAMILLE: I w-work hard to look after you – us -

THÉRÈSE: Your mother's money looks after us –

CAMILLE: We should be thinking of children!

THÉRÈSE: Have you been talking to her?

CAMILLE: Thérèse, why - why must everything be about my mother?

THÉRÈSE: She wants grandchildren.

CAMILLE: Thérèse, for for g-goodness sake!!

THÉRÈSE: (an abrupt about turn) Alright, come here.

CAMILLE: What?

THÉRÈSE: You're right.

CAMILLE: You - you really mean it? Or is this just another game?

THÉRÈSE: I married you, didn't I? Til death us do part? Let's get it over with.

Camille climbs into the bed, lies on top of Thérèse, as Laurent moves away afer sex. Thérèse shows no passion with Camille – is dead in the eyes. As he starts to fuck her, she leaves his crude embrace, his arms, watches him from the other side of the bed, returns to Laurent –

THÉRÈSE: You were here -
your breath on my body,
the breeze of you on my skin,
the rush of your coat past my sleeve,
the smell of you close,
the look of you, your eyes,
the curve of muscle,
the thought of your hands,
under my clothes
under your clothes the life of you,
your sweat, the hold of you, the whole of you, inside me I –
I –
I thought I -
I should die

Camille collapses, spent…

….Thérèse is embracing Laurent now, holding him, loving him, drunk with passion, the rhythm of their dance building, a year of passion rolled into one. Meanwhile Camille washes, self satisfied.

Suddenly Camille feels like the king of the world, like a small child in his triumph:

CAMILLE: Yes!

Simultaneously Laurent thinks he hears a noise. He's terrified he and Thérèse have been discovered.

Camille looks back at the bed, looks at the soiled sheets with mild distaste, then goes, happy as anything

LAURENT: Madame Raquin!
THÉRÈSE: Why would she come up? She's too scared of someone robbing the petty cash.

Thérèse tries to stop Laurent from dressing and leaving.

THÉRÈSE: Don't go.
LAURENT: Stop!
THÉRÈSE: Let her come. Hide if you want to. To hell with her! Let them all come!

Laurent is shocked. But now they both hear the footsteps on the stairs. Quickly Laurent grabs his waistcoat and hat. Thérèse laughs at how ridiculous he looks in his panic.

LAURENT: Thérèse!
THÉRÈSE: Here!

She quickly throws her petticoats over him, pushes him down onto the floor again. She throws on him anything else she can find, swiftly and without becoming flustered.

THÉRÈSE: Don't move!

Thérèse jumps into bed. She is half naked, her hair a mess, still flushed. Madame Raquin comes in, opening the door quietly and tiptoeing over.

MME RAQUIN: I thought I heard a noise. Are you ill?
THÉRÈSE: I'm sorry. I'll make it up to you tomorrow.
MME RAQUIN: Oh, my poor little Thérèse. (about to go, but…) Do you need anything?
THÉRÈSE: Just sleep, maman.

Again Madame Raquin is about to go, anxious about the shop, but can't resist:

MME RAQUIN: Thérèse, I know now might not be the best moment, but – You and Camille, you are - ?
THÉRÈSE: Happy?
MME RAQUIN: Only, if I can help in any way –
THÉRÈSE: Aunt, why should I not be happy? Your son is a stallion.

Madame Raquin is embarrassed by such talk.

MME RAQUIN: Yes, well - I – er - the way you treat Laurent, it's not right. If - if I've taught you anything, I hope I've taught you -
THÉRÈSE: To hide my true feelings.
MME RAQUIN: To show respect.
THÉRÈSE: Even if he's just here for what he can get.
MME RAQUIN: I don't need to remind you he's a friend of your husband's, a very good friend!
THÉRÈSE: Don't say I didn't warn you.
MME RAQUIN: Oh, don't be so ridiculous! Well: Camille will be home soon – he'll expect this place tidied up, really there's no excuse.

Madame Raquin leaves, avoiding confrontation. Laurent comes out of the covers.

LAURENT: My God, she's a monster!
THÉRÈSE: Who cares? She's blind.

Suddenly they hear a miaowing – a shadow at the window. Very quickly, Thérèse raises an arm and scares the cat away, almost before Laurent has had time to react.

THÉRÈSE: It's Francois you should worry about: he sees everything. He'll purr his secrets into Camille's ear one night –

LAURENT: OK -

THÉRÈSE: Don't underestimate him. 'Laurent and Thérèse's little affair makes me s-s-sick. Pleasssse lock them up so I can get a deccccent afternoon nap.'

Thérèse imitates the cat, stretching out her fingers like claws, rolling her shoulders. She snarls, ready to scratch Laurent's face. Laurent pulls back, a chill in his bones.

LAURENT: Don't! I should go before your husband returns.

THÉRÈSE: Coward.

LAURENT: It's risky enough getting to the back stairs without anyone seeing -

THÉRÈSE: I haven't finished with you -

LAURENT: Thérèse!

THÉRÈSE: God, why couldn't I have met you first?

LAURENT: But you didn't! If only we had! If only he weren't in the bloody -

He stops himself.

THÉRÈSE: In the way?

Silence.

LAURENT: You don't mean that.

THÉRÈSE: No, I don't. Do you?

For a long moment, Laurent looks at her. She stares back.

Nothing is said.

But when Laurent goes, he is even more uncertain than ever about her.

17.
Thérèse dresses, singing a love song, as downstairs another Thursday evening gathering begins to take place. The Doctor is there:

DOCTOR: Madame Raquin, my dear lady –
MME RAQUIN: Doctor!
DOCTOR: Seven o'clock on the dot, as usual. (hearing Thérèse upstairs) Someone's happy.
MME RAQUIN: Nothing wrong with having love in one's life, is there?

She looks to see the Doctor's reaction, but Camille enters. With Laurent.

MME RAQUIN: Laurent!
CAMILLE: I found him skulking like a criminal round the back!
LAURENT: A quiet smoke. Before coming up, I know you don't like the smell.
MME RAQUIN: Oh, Laurent, you're too perfect.

Thérèse enters in time to overhear the last line:

THÉRÈSE: Am I in the wrong house?
MME RAQUIN: Thérèse, please -
LAURENT: How are we today, Madame Raquin?
THÉRÈSE: Is that any of your business?

She turns her back on him.

CAMILLE: I must apologise.
LAURENT: She probably has some dark secret making her unhappy.
CAMILLE: No, I really d-don't think so –
LAURENT: Maybe you don't know her.
CAMILLE: Oh, I know everything about her.

Thérèse doesn't speak.

CAMILLE: Don't I, Thérèse?

Still no answer.

DOCTOR: Who's for a game of dominoes?
MME RAQUIN: Oh, good idea –
LAURENT: I'll fetch a bottle.
DOCTOR: Don't forget the glasses!

Laurent goes to get a bottle of red wine, as if he owns this place. Madame Raquin and the Doctor follow. Camille moves over to Thérèse, speaks to her quietly.

CAMILLE: Thérèse, it doesn't matter what you think of him, he's still my friend! Are you listening? Be welcoming!
THÉRÈSE: How welcoming?
CAMILLE: Good, you understand. I told Maman you would.

Although it is unclear to him if she does. Laurent is already back, with two bottles:

LAURENT: Two bottles're better than one!

MME RAQUIN: Oh, Laurent, you're so naughty!
CAMILLE: It's my turn to win!

Already they are pouring out the pieces onto the table, selecting, starting to play.

As they concentrate, Thérèse pulls Laurent away - the others don't even acknowledge them, once again they're in a different time, a different place: the kitchen.

LAURENT: We can't see each other anymore.
THÉRÈSE: What?
LAURENT: It's not what you think – The boss won't let me have any more time off.
THÉRÈSE: Liar!
LAURENT: I can't leave my desk every afternoon!
THÉRÈSE: Why not?
LAURENT: I'll lose my job!
THÉRÈSE: You haven't been near me for two weeks and now this – I'll leave him. Leave here!
LAURENT: You'd soon hate me. Where would we live?
THÉRÈSE: You've got someone else, haven't you?
LAURENT: You're not listening –
THÉRÈSE: (loud) If I can't have you, no one else will –
LAURENT: Keep your voice down!
THÉRÈSE: Who cares!
MME RAQUIN: (in the next door room) Are you coming back, Laurent?
LAURENT: (calling) Just on my way –
THÉRÈSE: You can't do this!
LAURENT: Thérèse, let me go!
THÉRÈSE: You belong to me!
LAURENT: Please – we'll talk –
THÉRÈSE: When?

LAURENT: Soon. Thérèse!!
MME RAQUIN: (calling at the same time) Thérèse?
THÉRÈSE: When??

Laurent looks terrified at her passion. Thérèse collapses to the floor. She grabs his ankles. Anything she can get hold of.

THÉRÈSE: (desperate) Don't leave me!!
LAURENT: I have to. Please. Understand. It's not my choice.
THÉRÈSE: No!!
LAURENT: I don't know what else to do!

Laurent pulls away, goes through to the other room. The others barely look up.

In the kitchen Thérèse is desolate.

18.
The party has dissolved.

Laurent walks home in torment. Passes other pedestrians, hurrying home. Knocks into a feeble looking man, a woman, another woman. Street lamps, the sound of horse-drawn carriages, a blind man. Laurent sees Thérèse everywhere. Every face is hers. She's on his skin, she's in his hair, she's everywhere. He claws at himself.

19.
Laurent ends up in his cramped attic apartment, alone.

No, she's here too! In his bed. It's late. The clock strikes eight. They're exhausted.

THÉRÈSE: I have to go.

Laurent doesn't react.

THÉRÈSE: See you again. One day.
LAURENT: Don't say that. Please. It's too uncertain. Thérèse?

Thérèse continues dressing.

LAURENT: Which day, when?
THÉRÈSE: I've no more excuses!
LAURENT: So this is it?
THÉRÈSE: No! I won't let it be! No!!

She changes her mind again.

THÉRÈSE: I'm going home –

Laurent stops her.

LAURENT: Can't you get rid of him? Send him on a trip! Anywhere!
THÉRÈSE: There's only one place you don't return from.

A moment's silence.

THÉRÈSE: But he'll see us to the grave first. People like him spend their entire lives at death's door – but they never die!

Laurent hugs Thérèse to him.

LAURENT: I had a dream. I spent the whole night with you, fell asleep in your arms, woke the next morning with your kisses on my lips... I want to be your husband. Do you understand, Thérèse? Do you understand what I'm saying?
THÉRÈSE: Oh Laurent, yes! Yes of course! Yes, yes, yes -

She shudders. Suddenly she covers his face with kisses. Crying.

THÉRÈSE: Tell me we'll see each other again.
LAURENT: So come back tomorrow!
THÉRÈSE: I can't! I've told you! I don't care for myself, but I can't destroy you!
LAURENT: If only Camille would just disappear!

Thérèse leaps to her feet. She stares at Laurent with a sombre look. Her lips begin to twitch. A long pause. Then she murmurs:

THÉRÈSE: People die.

Laurent doesn't reply. It's an appalling thing to say. Thérèse half-laughs, a momentary escaped hysteria.

LAURENT: It's no joke –
THÉRÈSE: I can't live without you -
LAURENT: Thérèse, no!
THÉRÈSE: No - ?

A pause. Laurent can barely speak.

LAURENT: A foot slips, a tile slides from a roof...

Now she says nothing.

LAURENT: If we can't see each other for a while, don't forget me.

Thérèse is about to leave. Quickly he catches her in his arms.

LAURENT: You're mine. Swear you'll give yourself to me, completely, body and soul, whenever I want.
THÉRÈSE: I belong to you, I breathe for you, do what you want with me, take what you want…I love you.

Just for a moment, they stay there, defiant. This is the first time she's told him.

Then they kiss passionately. Suddenly Thérèse tears herself from him, and runs away without looking back.

Laurent is alone. He sinks onto the bed, buries himself in the bed-sheet. Everything about it reminds him of Thérèse.

20.
The Doctor is with Madame Raquin and Camille.

DOCTOR: Perhaps we should organise a search party.
MME RAQUIN: I told her it was a wild goose chase.
CAMILLE: A debt is a debt, maman.
DOCTOR: The Rue de l'Ecole killer was never caught, you know?
MME RAQUIN: What?
DOCTOR: Nothing – sorry.
MME RAQUIN: Are you saying she's in danger?
DOCTOR: Oh no more than usual, the streets have always been full of murderers.
MME RAQUIN: You mean people like that aren't in

prison?

DOCTOR: Oh, some are never even suspects, madame.

MME RAQUIN: Impossible.

DOCTOR: Only yesterday I was talking to a good friend of mine, really quite high up in the police, you'd be surprised at the number of unsolved murders there are.

MME RAQUIN: Please, I prefer to believe the streets are safe –

DOCTOR: The police aren't infallible.

MME RAQUIN: But God sees!

DOCTOR: You remember the wagon driver who was cut to pieces. Whose body was found in various bags near Vernon – They never found his killer, did they? Not even with all that evidence. The murderer's probably a top magistrate by now. Or a priest! Oh, don't look so alarmed, you're more likely to be run down by a coach than chopped up.

Just then Thérèse comes back.

DOCTOR: There she is! See: I told you everything would be fine.

MME RAQUIN: Where have you been?

CAMILLE: You've been out hours!

They wait for Thérèse's explanation.

THÉRÈSE: They said she'd be in, so I waited. Since I'd gone all that way - I thought I should at least try to collect the money. Of course, she never appeared. Then a woman in the apartment next to hers told me she'd moved three days ago –

MME RAQUIN: You obtained a forwarding address?

THÉRÈSE: Oh. Of course I should have done -

DOCTOR: (rescuing her without realising) Poor Thérèse,

you look done in. You should go straight to bed. As shall I –
Bon nuit, one and all.

The Doctor leaves. Immediately they close in on Thérèse.

MME RAQUIN: I told you it was a fool's errand!
CAMILLE: (at the same time) It's your own fault for not
listening!
THÉRÈSE: I'm going to bed.
CAMILLE: You haven't even said hello -

Suddenly Thérèse attacks Camille. Slow, haunting. Camille
doesn't notice, in a different world.

At the same moment, Laurent, in his attic, twists the sheet
into a tourniquet:

LAURENT: I'll kill him.

21.
A riverbank forms around them, the sound of water. Laurent,
Camille and Thérèse arrive for a picnic. Thérèse holds
Camille's arm. Camille fans himself with a handkerchief.

Laurent follows lazily behind, hatless.

A blazing hot day, a Seurat landscape, happy, light, bright
sunshine. A reddish layer of leaves cover the ground.

LAURENT: Here ?
CAMILLE: It seems dry…

Camille gets ready to place his coat tails down so he can sit
on them.

THÉRÈSE: Do we have to stop?

Laurent gives her a fierce look, unseen by Camille.

CAMILLE: Laurent likes it.
THÉRÈSE: And we have to do what Laurent says now?
CAMILLE: Is this why you barely see us any more, Laurent? Because of my wife's rudeness?
LAURENT: Your wife knows her own mind, don't you, Madame Raquin?

Laurent tries to stop her with his eyes.

LAURENT: Well, are we stopping here or not?
THÉRÈSE: Too many people.
CAMILLE: Where?
THÉRÈSE: You don't see them?
CAMILLE: Down by the water? They're miles away!
LAURENT: Who'd want to watch us?
CAMILLE: Well, I'm going to lie right here.

Camille does so. He continues to fan his face.

Thérèse too lies down. She is half disappointed, half relieved.

The sound of rowers passing. Far off voices out for a Sunday stroll. Crickets in the heat. Murmurings. For a moment all is peaceful, as Laurent watches but cannot touch.

Then Laurent too lays down. Near Thérèse. Out of sight of Camille, he puts his lips to Thérèse's boot. Then he puts his hand up her skirt. Thérèse tries to fight him off lightly but enjoys what he is doing.

Camille's hand droops. He hat tilts down over his eyes, he talks with eyes closed:

CAMILLE: A perfect day.

Thérèse laughs. Camille can't see what's going on from his position.

CAMILLE: I'm serious -
THÉRÈSE: No, something's tickling my leg. A pest -
CAMILLE: Then kill it.

Camille dozes off, starts to snore gently.

A rowing crew are heard passing, the stroke calling out the sculling speed.

Laurent continues. His hand moves further up inside Thérèse's dress. Thérèse begins to move to the rhythm of Laurent's fingers, when Laurent takes his hand away, stands up. He looks down on her, then very deliberately goes to the sleeping Camille. He stands over him, then raises his heel, as if he is about to bring it down on Camille's head.

THÉRÈSE: (panicking) No!
CAMILLE: (waking) What? What is it?
LAURENT: A wasp in your hair -
THÉRÈSE: Nothing, go back to sleep –
CAMILLE: (clawing himself) Ugh! Let's leave!
LAURENT: It's gone.
CAMILLE: Let's go on the water!
THÉRÈSE: No!

LAURENT: Good idea -

THÉRÈSE: Your mother said you weren't to –

CAMILLE: I have to do what she says, do I?

LAURENT: Quite right, Camille, you do exactly as you want.

THÉRÈSE: It's not safe!

LAURENT: So we'll take good care of you, won't we? Won't we, Thérèse?

The bright day is turning to dusk. Ominous clouds. Lanterns on the riverbank. Distant lights. Immense sheets of pale light on the reddening trees and white roads.

THÉRÈSE: It's going to rain. Let's go home.

LAURENT: Let the rain come down.

CAMILLE: Come on, let's hire a boat before it's too late!

THÉRÈSE: It's already late.

LAURENT: Nonsense. Just for an hour or so. (To Camille) You deserve a break from the monotony of timetables. (To Thérèse) Did you hear, another one derailed last week. Seven people injured and two dead! Fourth disaster in three years, no one's safe. And the bosses got a reward! A huge payout for killing innocent people!

22.

The boat appears. Camille is a little drunk, doesn't notice Laurent whisper to Thérèse.

LAURENT: Just do as I say…

The shadows lengthen. Death lurks. Laurent jumps into the narrow skiff, Camille hesitates:

LAURENT: (laughing) Come on, in you get. Coward.

Laurent helps Camille in. Camille wobbles his way to the stern, where he sits down.

LAURENT: Thérèse.
THÉRÈSE: I'm not coming.
CAMILLE: Come on -
LAURENT: You must -
CAMILLE: Thérèse, I order you!! I - I refuse to go without you!
LAURENT: Just get in the boat.
CAMILLE: Look at her, she's the one who's scared.
LAURENT: Now or never.

Thérèse hesitates. Laurent starts to push off – then at the last moment:

THÉRÈSE: I'm coming!
CAMILLE: Women!

Thérèse lands awkwardly, but Laurent rights her. He looks at her hard – she gives nothing away, stays in the bow. They take the boat out.

Peace. Thérèse breathes heavily. Camille dips his hand in.

CAMILLE: It's freezing!

Laurent looks at Thérèse, unseen by Camille. Camille rests his elbows on either side of the boat, lolling. Laurent stops rowing. He rubs his large strong hands on his knees, his lips tighten.

Then Laurent rocks the boat.

CAMILLE: Oh!
THÉRÈSE: You're not scared by a little rocking, are you, poor little Camille?
CAMILLE: Don't –
LAURENT: Poor you. Christ, I remember, you used to be so scared of water you wouldn't even let your mother wash your hair!

Thérèse laughs.

CAMILLE: Rubbish!

The sound of water in the background builds, ominous. Distant fireworks can be heard.

CAMILLE: Is that a weir? Let's go back.
LAURENT: Don't move so much.
CAMILLE: It's too dark -
LAURENT: Isn't it wonderful? Nothing but stars. It's perfect.
CAMILLE: I love you like a brother, Laurent. You're the truest friend I've ever had.
THÉRÈSE: (dragging her hand in the water) Perfect.

Thérèse casually splashes Camille with water.

CAMILLE: Don't.

Thérèse splashes him again.

CAMILLE: What are you doing, stupid? Stop it.
THÉRÈSE: It's only water.

Laurent sits beside Camille, puts his arms round him.

CAMILLE: Don't, that tickles! Come on, let's go home before someone falls in! Laurent, I'm serious, I can't swim!

Laurent grips harder. Camille turns to look at him, and suddenly sees the contorted expression on Laurent's face. For the first time, he realises his predicament –

CAMILLE: Laurent, what are you doing?

Laurent starts to squeeze Camille's neck now. Camille struggles. Tries to scurry away across the bottom of the boat, on his hands and knees.

CAMILLE: Thérèse, help me!

Thérèse does nothing. Laurent is relentless. Grabs Camille again, wrenches him away from the boat. Slowly lifts him. At the last moment, Camille twists round and sinks his teeth deep into Laurent's neck.

LAURENT: Ow!

And then suddenly Laurent has thrown Camille overboard.

THÉRÈSE: – oh! –

Thérèse looks at Laurent, who clutches his neck. Laurent stares back at her.

Camille is gone.

Suddenly Camille erupts back up to the surface. He screams.

CAMILLE: Help me, Thérèse. Thérèse!

Thérèse sits stock still. Paralysed. Camille disappears again. Laurent sees Thérèse do nothing. Then, suddenly, the boat rocks: Camille's gripping the side of the boat... Laurent unlocks Camille's fingers, holds him down. Thérèse does nothing. Camille soaked, reaches his hands up, Laurent holds him down. Screams, pitiful...

CAMILLE: (half underwater) Help me, Thérèse -

And then he's gone.

A sudden eruption of fireworks in the distance.

Thérèse is in shock. She reaches her arms out, almost too quiet to hear:

THÉRÈSE: Hold me.
LAURENT: Thérèse, they'll see us!! Quick, turn the boat over!
THÉRÈSE: Hold me -

Some oarsmen can be heard rowing down the river in the distance.

THÉRÈSE: Oh God, what have we done?
LAURENT: What had to be done.

Laurent looks at Thérèse.

LAURENT: Now, Thérèse!

She nods.

LAURENT: (loud, calling) Help! Help over here!

Thérèse and Camille silhouetted, the sound of the water deafening.

They leap.

END OF ACT ONE

ACT TWO

1.
Someone is being drowned in the water, even if we can't see the face. It is harsh, brutal. They are left for dead.

Simultaneously, Thérèse is seen in bed, feverish.

2.
Meanwhile Madame Raquin is with the Doctor.

MME RAQUIN: There's no proof. He could be anywhere! Any minute he could walk in through the door.

Just at that moment, Camille is seen – alive. Again, his face isn't seen.

MME RAQUIN: See! I told you, I knew it! Oh my poor little Camille, you're alive!

Thérèse starts up in panic. Instantly Camille is gone. Madame Raquin is distraught.

MME RAQUIN: Oh God, oh God, oh God, oh God -
DOCTOR: Laurent tried to save your son, they both did. He was dancing in the boat. They might all have drowned. Laurent jumped in to save him.
MME RAQUIN: I nursed him for so many years, I brought him back into the world at least a dozen times -
DOCTOR: Madame Raquin –
MME RAQUIN: And now you say he's dead, far away, in dirty cold water, like a dog, no, it's not true -
DOCTOR: Shh, shhh now –

MME RAQUIN: Like a dog!

3.
Laurent is with Thérèse in her room, awkward.

LAURENT: Thérèse. My darling?

Laurent reaches for her hand. She instinctively pulls it back.

THÉRÈSE: What's happened to your voice?

Laurent reaches again and this time she lets him hold it. But he doesn't kiss her.

LAURENT: Be strong. Don't forget.
THÉRÈSE: How can I!
LAURENT: I'm here. With you. For always.

He starts to leave.

THÉRÈSE: Where are you going?
LAURENT: I can't stay here, we must wait -
THÉRÈSE: Have they found the body?

Laurent doesn't answer.

THÉRÈSE: They have to find my husband's body!

And it is Thérèse who is gone. Laurent is left alone.

4.
Laurent looks into a mirror. He undoes a scarf, turns down his high shirt collar, and studies the wound on his neck – a

red gash below the right ear, where the skin's been torn to reveal pinkish flesh. Trickles of blood have run down to his shoulder and now hardened.

Laurent leans forward to see more clearly, his face twitches, and then contorts into a horrible grimace. He hides the wound once more, and leaves.

5.
At the same time, a series of horrible faces are seen: bodies in the morgue, ranged against the wall, as if on vertical slabs, pathetic rags of trousers and skirts and bodies grimly contorted against the bare plaster.

Laurent arrives to visit the morgue. The pale sickly smell turns his stomach. He presses his face forward, to see Camille.

The chorus of morgue bodies become a society group looking at the bodies, nosy, laughing, coming forward towards Laurent. He flees.

6.
Back in their flat, Madame Raquin tortures herself, as the Doctor looks on helplessly. The chorus become morgue figures again, floating in space around her, ever more grotesque.

MME RAQUIN: I should never have let him go.
DOCTOR: It's not your fault, Madame Raquin.
MME RAQUIN: I knew he was afraid of the water –
DOCTOR: It was an accident. Perhaps the body's trapped

somewhere. Under a bridge?

Laurent arrives.

LAURENT: He's not in the morgue.
DOCTOR: Laurent, you've done all you can –
LAURENT: Why did I take him out? If I'd only known he couldn't swim –
DOCTOR: Didn't you?

Laurent looks terrified, has he been caught out? But the Doctor thinks he's suffering:

DOCTOR: No, no, of course not. Why would you?
LAURENT: I'll never forgive myself!
DOCTOR: You did your best, yes? Dived in to save him – no friend could have done more.

7.
Suddenly Camille's body rolls forward, fast – bloated, hardly dressed, drowned. It's shocking: the lips are twisted in a horrible sneer; the blackish tip of the tongue pokes between white teeth, the head is stretched and tanned like leather, hair plastered against the temples, the body battered, shrunk. The ribs make black stripes across the greenish chest. There is a jagged hole on the left side of the body, with dark red edges. The legs are covered in blotches.

LAURENT: (almost whispered) Oh my God -

Laurent slowly retreats, sickened and horrified by the sight.

8.

As Laurent sees Camille, Thérèse gets up from her bed. She brushes her hair, with a kind of feverish resolve. She sits for a while with her hands on her temples, staring straight ahead, apparently lost in thought.

She jumps out of bed, dresses herself with hurried, trembling movements. She goes to look at herself in the mirror, rubs her eyes and runs her hands over her face is if to wipe something away. Then, without uttering a word, she goes through to Madame Raquin, dreading their first encounter since the death.

The two women stare at each other, Thérèse with growing anxiety, Madame Raquin making painful efforts to remember. At last Madame Raquin holds out her trembling arms, as Thérèse did on the boat.

MME RAQUIN: Dear, dear Thérèse.
THÉRÈSE: I'm sorry.

Madame Raquin puts her arms round Thérèse's neck, enveloping her.

9.
LAURENT: We've found the body.

Laurent is there.

Madame Raquin doesn't react. They wait to see what she will do. Gradually, very slowly, she gets up. It is clear she's aged considerably. Her hair has whitened. She needs a walking stick to drag herself into the dining room. She moves heavily, pausing on each step. Laurent can't look at Thérèse.

MME RAQUIN: It's time to reopen the shop.

Madame Raquin starts to cry.

MME RAQUIN: You're all I have left in the world!
DOCTOR: Madame Raquin, try not to get so upset, you'll only make yourself ill. Crying won't bring your son back. You'll upset Thérèse. And the rest of us. Perhaps we should play a game?

Laurent looks at Thérèse. But she is impassive. Madame Raquin's in no state to say anything.

LAURENT: Yes, let's play.

The Doctor gets the dominoes.

10.
As they play, the Doctor puts down Madame Raquin's pieces for her. Thérèse circles the table. The game and argument are in different times:

LAURENT: Thérèse. We have to talk –
THÉRÈSE: I'm busy.
LAURENT: Busy!
THÉRÈSE: With the shop.
LAURENT: Since when have you ever cared about the shop?
THÉRÈSE: She needs my help.
LAURENT: Thérèse –

THÉRÈSE: She's just lost her only son!
LAURENT: And we know why -
THÉRÈSE: I can't sit still anymore. My hands jump. This is torture!

The game continues, everyone now in the same world. Thérèse plays too.

Doctor: You're looking much better, Madame Raquin. Isn't she looking well? A bit of colour in those cheeks. Time's a great healer. (she's crying) Oh now, dear Madame Raquin, please. Life must go on.

He gives her a big smile.

Time slips by inexorably. as the dominoes continue, Thérèse and Laurent talk, a different world.

THÉRÈSE: Laurent, you know we must wait. If we're to be together –
LAURENT: You want us to be, do you?
THÉRÈSE: I'm a widow. In mourning. What did you expect?
LAURENT: (under his breath) Christ, I must have been drunk!
THÉRÈSE: What?
LAURENT: Nothing –
THÉRÈSE: You said –
LAURENT: It was nothing, I told you!
THÉRÈSE: Drunk? Is that all I was to you?!
LAURENT: Don't you dare! I risked the guillotine for you! For what? You won't come near me!
THÉRÈSE: And when did we last see you?
LAURENT: I've been busy.

THÉRÈSE: Doing what?

He doesn't answer.

THÉRÈSE: Painting nudes?

He still doesn't answer.

THÉRÈSE: Do you love me?
LAURENT: Quiet! Anyone could be listening.
THÉRÈSE: You've never once said you loved me –
LAURENT: I'm tired of waiting!

Thérèse's hands and face are on fire. She can't stay still. Both of them are heart-broken, but trying not to show it. Laurent leaves abruptly.

11.
As Laurent heads home, he thinks he sees someone watching. Eyes seems to stare at him as he goes, pursuing him, whichever direction he goes in. Large shadows loom. The sounds of the night startle him.

He undoes his collar, the red wound is revealed. He rubs at it. It hurts more, not less.

Footsteps suddenly hurtle past him. He jumps, really shaky now.

LAURENT: What do you want with me?!

There's no one there.

A pool of light appears up ahead of him. He has to go

through the light, but feels terrified. A huge shadow looms up:

It's Camille.

Laurent flees.

12.
Alone, Thérèse gets ready for bed. She washes, soaks her face, obsessively trying to clean herself of her guilt…

when suddenly the dead Camille heads towards her. She tries to escape, shrinks back horrified, as he spews out sickly green river water from his mouth - bile.

Thérèse freaks, as Camille vanishes.

13.
Laurent has come to see Thérèse. He meets Madame Raquin first:

MME RAQUIN: Poor Thérèse had a bad night. Nightmares. And terrible trouble getting back to sleep. I heard her cry out. She's not at all well this morning.

As Madame Raquin speaks, Thérèse appears behind her. She looks shattered: feverish and downcast. She stares hard at Laurent.

LAURENT: Madame Raquin tells me you didn't sleep.
THÉRÈSE: Oh, she exaggerates. I was hot, that's all –
LAURENT: It is hot, isn't it?
THÉRÈSE: At night especially –

LAURENT: It'll pass soon.
THÉRÈSE: Let us hope so.

As they speak in banalities, Camille appears behind Madame Raquin and laughs at them – soundless, black mouthed. Both of them shiver simultaneously, unaware.

THÉRÈSE: Shut the window, Aunt, I'm cold.
MME RAQUIN: Cold? But you just said -

Instantly Thérèse and Laurent have moved to another time. Madame Raquin's gone.

LAURENT: We must get married.
THÉRÈSE: What's the hurry?
LAURENT: You see him too, don't you?
THÉRÈSE: I don't know what you're talking about -
LAURENT: Camille.
THÉRÈSE: No!

Thérèse moves forward to kiss Laurent, almost a repeat of their first passionate embrace. But this time he pushes her off. He's frantic.

LAURENT: I see him everywhere! I can't go up the stairs, he's waiting for me! I lock all the doors, check under the bed. We can't be apart now, we have to be together, it's the only way to get rid of him!

He stops exhausted. They don't touch. Finally she speaks.

THÉRÈSE: Everything we do must be above suspicion.

14.

Thérèse looks sad. The Doctor watches her, with Madame Raquin:

MME RAQUIN: She's withdrawn into herself. Stopped eating. She wanders round the house all night long like a ghost; after more than a year, it's not right.
DOCTOR: I'll take another look.
MME RAQUIN: I don't want her to die.
DOCTOR: But – Madame Raquin, her illness - Well, it's – in my opinion, she is not so much physically ill -
MME RAQUIN: You don't think you can die of grief!

The Doctor doesn't know how to answer. Time slides.

DOCTOR: Madame Raquin, you may not wish to hear this.
MME RAQUIN: Tell me.
DOCTOR: I've noticed – It's been a long time… eighteen months since her husband's - accident.
MME RAQUIN: I think about him every day, may his soul rest in peace –
DOCTOR: I should say no more -
MME RAQUIN: I want her cured! I couldn't bear to lose both of them.
DOCTOR: (delicate) The remedy could perhaps be easy.
MME RAQUIN: Yes - ?
DOCTOR: In my opinion your niece is… bored.
MME RAQUIN: Bored?
DOCTOR: She's been alone a long time.

Madame Raquin is clearly hurt by this.

DOCTOR: I'm sorry to say this. But she needs a companion. Male company. As soon as possible.

Madame Raquin is in tears.

The Doctor is replaced by Laurent.

LAURENT: Do you need anything, Madame Raquin? You want me to sit with you? Perhaps I could mind the till while you go out for fresh air? Or I could bring some small cakes -

Laurent notices that Thérèse is staring at him in an odd way. He stops abruptly.

MME RAQUIN: Laurent, you're so kind. You're like a perfect son.

Back to the Doctor and Madame Raquin. They study Laurent.

DOCTOR: There's the man your niece needs. You must fix the marriage as soon as you can.
MME RAQUIN: Marriage?
DOCTOR: It's perfect. It's the perfect match.

15.
The Doctor's with Laurent.

LAURENT: Marriage?
DOCTOR: You must admit it's the perfect solution.
LAURENT: Doctor, I admit I'm very fond of the two women, but - she's... she's like a – a sister to me. It would feel... wrong. Immoral even -
DOCTOR: Laurent, there are a hundred good reasons why you might attach yourself to her, yes? She's not unattractive. She's a widow. You're her only friend. You were her

husband's best friend. You're much loved by Madame Raquin. By both ladies.

The Doctor's getting nowhere. Laurent just seems bewildered.

DOCTOR: You're a true friend to the family. They're devoted to you. In the eyes of God, you'd be making a noble sacrifice!

The Doctor continues but we no longer hear what he says.

16.
Madame Raquin is with Thérèse. Thérèse is about to go to bed. She is frail.

MME RAQUIN: Thérèse –
THÉRÈSE: Yes, Aunt.
MME RAQUIN: Are you happy?
THÉRÈSE: Happy?
MME RAQUIN: I know life has been…difficult for you, recently.
THÉRÈSE: No more for me than you.
MME RAQUIN: The life of a widow can be… lonely.
THÉRÈSE: We've plenty of distractions – the shop -
MME RAQUIN: Do you not long for…more intimate company?
THÉRÈSE: Aunt, I don't know what you're trying to say -
MME RAQUIN: Thérèse, please don't be offended when I say this, but –

Thérèse looks uncomfortable. Madame Raquin jumps in before Thérèse can stop her.

MME RAQUIN: You're not too young to marry again.
THÉRÈSE: Marry! Oh God, no -
MME RAQUIN: You never had a chance –
THÉRÈSE: He's only just dead!
MME RAQUIN: It's been nearly two years, Thérèse!
THÉRÈSE: No! I can't!
MME RAQUIN: You could still have children. You need to think of the future, your future -
THÉRÈSE: I have no future!
MME RAQUIN: This despair can't go on for ever!
THÉRÈSE: Aunt, I could never replace him, Camille was everything to me!
MME RAQUIN: (crying again, but not about to stop) What about Laurent?
THÉRÈSE: Laurent!

Thérèse seems gob-smacked.

MME RAQUIN: It's a good match. You're well suited, he's a good kind sweet man. You know him already, he won't disrupt our life here. He's charming, honest. Any woman would be proud to get him! But not you. I'm warning you, Thérèse, you're lucky this is even being considered!

Madame Raquin realises she's gone too far. Thérèse looks horrified.

MME RAQUIN: No, I didn't mean – Thérèse, my dearest child, my only wish is to grow old with the two of you by my side. And you need to live once more. At least consider my words.
THÉRÈSE: I love Laurent only as a brother.

Madame Raquin gives up.

THÉRÈSE: But – for you - I'll try to love him like a husband.
MME RAQUIN: Oh! Oh, Thérèse, you don't know how happy you make me.
THÉRÈSE: I'd been hoping to mourn a little longer.
MME RAQUIN: Oh, Thérèse, I didn't mean -
THÉRÈSE: My only wish is to make you happy.

Thérèse kisses Madame Raquin who is overcome by astonishment. Thérèse leaves.

Madame Raquin is left alone. Suddenly she realises what she's done.

MME RAQUIN: Oh Camille, please forgive me, little Camille, if you're there – please, I haven't forgotten you, poor darling Camille, I haven't!

17.
The Doctor and Laurent join Thérèse and Madame Raquin. The Doctor thinks he is talking quietly:

DOCTOR: He accepts!
MME RAQUIN: Oh that's wonderful.

Thérèse hears. She looks hard at Laurent, and he stares back, as if asking each other advice. Then as if a decision has been made, Laurent goes to Madame Raquin, and takes her hand.

LAURENT: Dear mother -
MME RAQUIN: Oh!

Hearing herself called 'dear mother' sets Madame Raquin off. She seizes Thérèse's hand and puts it in Laurent's, unable to speak. The two lovers feel a shiver as their skin touches. They keep their fingers tightly intertwined.

LAURENT: Thérèse, you will make your Aunt's life happy.
THÉRÈSE: We must fulfil our duty.
LAURENT: I couldn't tell anyone before. When Camille fell in, his last words were: 'Save my wife, I leave her in your hands.'
THÉRÈSE: No!
MME RAQUIN: (nearly fainting) Oh –
LAURENT: I believe, by marrying her, I shall be carrying out his dying wishes.

Thérèse lets go of Laurent's hand. Madame Raquin thinks Thérèse is upset.

MME RAQUIN: Laurent, my dear friend! Yes, do marry her – my son will thank you from the depths of his grave.
DOCTOR: Come on, you two, kiss to mark the engagement!

Laurent kisses Thérèse on the cheek. She recoils, as if his lips burn.

DOCTOR: Look, she's shy. Bit late for that, eh? (he laughs heartily) New blood, that's all that's needed round here!

Thérèse and Laurent look at each other, smile weakly. Madame Raquin smiles too, even if feeling guilty about Camille. The Doctor rubs his hands in glee.

DOCTOR: This was all my idea, you know... and look at

you now! Just see what a fine young couple you'll make! And what a wedding! Who shall we invite? Your father!

LAURENT: He won't come. He disowned me, didn't he? Made it perfectly clear I'm to stand on my own two feet. Didn't I tell you? I can't pretend it's not been difficult, but you have to make your own way in life, don't you?

DOCTOR: (awkward, then) Good for you, boy, good for you.

MME RAQUIN: In that case – I've an important announcement: now you two dear children are getting married, I've decided to make over to my niece… my entire worldly capital!

DOCTOR: Madame Raquin!

MME RAQUIN: Oh, I'll still have the profits from the shop.

LAURENT: Madame Raquin, you're too generous. Really – how can we ever repay you?

MME RAQUIN: Nonsense, you've repaid me already, Laurent. Many times over. You love me. I love you. You've more than proved it today by this - this arrangement. There'll be plenty of money for all of us. You can be happy and secure in your new marriage. It's good.

Thérèse and Laurent look at each other uncertainly.

18.

For a moment, there's the possibility of hope: Laurent and Thérèse's wedding repeats Camille and Thérèse's, with slight variations: Thérèse is dressed again – this time fast. She comes down to join Laurent. Madame Raquin and the Doctor are there too.

CHORUS: Pour nous aimer fidelement

Dans le bonheur ou dans les epreuves
Et nous soutenir l'un l'autre
Tout au long de notre vie

DOCTOR: A toast. To the children of Laurent and Thérèse.

As the bedroom appears, the chorus throw down cankered petals. The mood is increasingly diseased.

CHORUS: For richer, for poorer
For better, for worse
In sickness and in health
Til death do us part

19.
Laurent and Thérèse enter the bedroom, side by side, but not touching. But they've got through the first ordeal:

LAURENT: See, Thérèse, that wasn't so difficult, was it? Just close your eyes, and everything turns out all right.

Thérèse sees the wedding bed – it brings everything back – it almost makes her sick. The room feels diseased.

THÉRÈSE: Sorry, I feel –
LAURENT: We've drunk too much!
THÉRÈSE: I didn't drink –
LAURENT: Thérèse, my wife!
THÉRÈSE: (hearing a scratching) What's that?
LAURENT: Nothing.

They listen.

LAURENT: Kiss me.

Thérèse can't relax, tries to kiss Laurent, he offers her his livid red neck. She recoils.

THÉRÈSE: No – I –

She hears the scratching again.

THÉRÈSE: What is that noise?
LAURENT: Don't - Forget him! He's gone.

Laurent makes a grab for her.

THÉRÈSE: Wash first.
LAURENT: Wash?
THÉRÈSE: I want to remember our wedding night with pleasure.

Laurent staggers to the washing bowl – washes, then dips his head right in. For a moment, he looks like a drowned man. Laurent strips off his shirt. Behind him, Thérèse shows no pleasure.

Camille is there too, in the shadows.

CAMILLE: Scrub my back.

Thérèse flinches, looks around the bedroom.

LAURENT: Thérèse –

He tries to kiss her, she sidesteps him.

LAURENT: Come to bed.
THÉRÈSE: I need to wash.

LAURENT/CAMILLE: After -
THÉRÈSE: I'm dirty now. And tired. What a day.
LAURENT/CAMILLE: And what a night it'll be.

Thérèse is confused by the repetitions of Camille's words. She's entered her own hell. She hears Camille, but can't see him.

LAURENT: Come to bed -
CAMILLE: Come to bed -

Thérèse stalling for time, washing obsessively. Laurent watches her, moves towards her.

THÉRÈSE: In a minute - one minute only, Laurent, grant me that -
LAURENT: Do you remember our afternoons in this room?

Laurent's hesitant, unsure what to do. Thérèse turns to the fire, hunches.

LAURENT: I used to dream of spending the whole night with you.

Thérèse shudders at the memory.

THÉRÈSE: Go to bed. Keep yourself warm.
LAURENT: We've done it, Thérèse. We're free.
THÉRÈSE: (hearing the scratching again) Camille - ?

Laurent stops short, unable to carry on. They stare at each other, pale and shaking. Laurent moves towards her.

THÉRÈSE: It's hot. It's too hot. Is there no air in here?

LAURENT: Thérèse, we're safe now –
THÉRÈSE: We need more wood for the fire.
LAURENT: You said you were too hot –
THÉRÈSE: There's a draft, coming from under the – under the door. It's so quiet…

The yellow light of the fire dances away across the walls and ceiling. Thérèse can stall no longer – her look of dread is unseen by Laurent as he gets into bed.

THÉRÈSE: I'm so cold. Oh God, what have we done?
LAURENT: Stop! That's enough!

Thérèse goes towards the bed. She climbs in. Laurent climbs on top of her, tries to undo her clothes –

THÉRÈSE: What are you doing?
LAURENT: I'm – you're my wife now –
THÉRÈSE: I'll do it!

Thérèse pushes Laurent off. Then she undoes her garments. Again Laurent climbs on top of her. At first he's rough, desperate to get rid of the ghost of Camille.

THÉRÈSE: Wait, that hurts!

And then Laurent starts to cough, convulsively

THÉRÈSE: Camille, no!

Thérèse pushes him off. Laurent looks at her with bewilderment. She sees his look: he's about to hit her. She cowers. He manages to hold back, hits the pillow instead.

THÉRÈSE: Oh, God. Laurent, I'm sorry. (hearing the

scratching again) He's here! Camille's here!
LAURENT: Camille can go to hell! He's dead, forget him!

Suddenly loud caterwauling is heard. Thérèse and Laurent jump.

THÉRÈSE: Oh!

Thérèse goes to the window. Emptiness – then for the briefest of moments, Camille's shadow the full height of the theatre - before she slams the shutters closed.

THÉRÈSE: God, it's so cold!

Laurent can't touch her.

The chorus gather, vultures. The blind man tapping his cane relentlessly. Camille in the distance, barely distinguishable among them. The glint of a knife.

20.
Doctor and Madame Raquin are delighting in the marriage they engineered, over a drink.

DOCTOR: You must be very happy, dear Madame Raquin.
MME RAQUIN: Tired but happy.
DOCTOR: I haven't been up this late in years. Must try it more often! Oh, but I'm keeping you from your own bed.
MME RAQUIN: It wouldn't have happened without you –
DOCTOR: Well, I don't know where I'd go every Thursday if not for this place! You have a wonderful family.

The Doctor is getting up to go. Finally Madame Raquin makes her move.

MME RAQUIN: (putting her arm on him) You could stay –
DOCTOR: What? It's late, Madame Raquin.
MME RAQUIN: Yes, of course, but
DOCTOR: I should tell you about my girl in blue.
MME RAQUIN: Pardon?
Doctor: Sorry, was going to wait. Sorry. I er… I have a telescope. To watch the world go by. From my roof-top flat. The most magnificent views in all Paris. I like to think so. From the gutter to the stars…
MME RAQUIN: You've lost me.
DOCTOR: I saw a girl. In a blue dress – I wasn't looking – just tilted down to get my bearings and… now I rather think I'm in love with her.
MME RAQUIN: In love? With a woman you haven't met!
DOCTOR: I know, I don't even know where she lives! I mean, I know where she lives as the crow flies, but what street, what street number, what apartment – no idea! Madame Raquin, I'm pining.
MME RAQUIN: But you're a confirmed bachelor!
DOCTOR: Isn't love wonderful? And surprising. I mean, at my age. 'No longer a passion hidden out of sight, Now that Goddess Venus holds me tight.' Racine!
MME RAQUIN: You don't know her!
DOCTOR: Ah, but who knows anyone? Even couples who've been married for years. Come now, we all have our secrets, I'm sure?

Madame Raquin is flabbergasted, disturbed, upset.

21.
Thérèse and Laurent are far apart, Thérèse staring into the fire. Laurent marooned in the bed.

THÉRÈSE: You're sure it was him at the morgue?
LAURENT: We really have to go over this again?
THÉRÈSE: Did it - it look as if he'd suffered?
LAURENT: Kiss me.

Thérèse looks terribly pale in her night-dress. She sees his neck.

THÉRÈSE: I didn't know you'd hurt yourself.
LAURENT: This? It's…nothing –
THÉRÈSE: Teeth marks!

A long pause.

LAURENT: Camille - bit me. It's, it's - all right now…it's healing.
THÉRÈSE: It was two years ago!
LAURENT: It… it comes back.

Thérèse can't believe what she's hearing.

LAURENT: K-kiss me, kiss me, please!

He is beginning to sound a bit like Camille. He offers his neck, Thérèse pulls away in horror.

THÉRÈSE: No, anywhere but there!

Thérèse slumps down. Laurent stands uncomprehendingly. Then suddenly he moves towards her, fast, grabs her head in his hands, pushing her lips towards his scar.

Revolted, Thérèse tries to pull away, but he holds her fast, forcing her lips onto him. She can barely breathe. Finally she manages to escape, retching. She wipes her lips violently and spits.

LAURENT: Look, we chucked him in because he was a nuisance! And we'd chuck him in again, wouldn't we? So stop being so childish! When we're all dead and buried, the fact we shoved some idiot in the Seine won't make a blind bit of difference to anyone! But we'll have spent our lives together. So kiss me.

Thérèse does finally kiss him, frigid and panic-stricken. She shakes.

THÉRÈSE: (desperate) Oh, hold me, Laurent, hold me!

The portrait of Camille seems to move. Laurent sees it, looks as if he'll be sick

LAURENT: He's there! Take it down.
THÉRÈSE: What?
LAURENT: He's watching us!
THÉRÈSE: I can't. She'll know. They'll know. Everyone will know!

They hear the scratching sound again. Then more scratching. They're both terrified. Suddenly Laurent rushes out of the room. As the door opens, the cat's heard -

THÉRÈSE: No, don't hurt him!

A thump, the cat cries in agony. Simultaneously a splash of red across the back wall. The cat can be heard dying. The noise is hideous. Thérèse sings to blot it out.

THÉRÈSE: Sur le pont d'Avignon, On y danse on y danse. Sur le pont d'Avignon, On y danse on y danse. Sur le pont d'Avignon, On y danse on y danse -

Laurent returns – his hand is scratched and bleeding. Thérèse looks at him in horror.

LAURENT: New blood in the family.

Laurent laughs: nasty, subdued hysteria.

Thérèse starts her song again.

22.
The Doctor is with Madame Raquin. Increasingly during the rest of the play this outside world invades Thérèse and Laurent's shrinking bedroom:

DOCTOR: You'll never guess. I've found her! My girl in blue. I worked from a map, measured as accurately as I could how many streets away she might be, took my bearings from a large church not far from her apartment. You can see the steeple from my window -
MME RAQUIN: I'm worried about Thérèse –
DOCTOR: Thérèse, why?
MME RAQUIN: She has such dark shadows under her eyes.
DOCTOR: She's only just married, what did you expect! I mean, it has to be said, poor sickly Camille was never, well, he can never have been very much of a husband, yes? Sorry to speak so bluntly, Madame Raquin, but I'm afraid it's true: where were the children?
MME RAQUIN: You think that's all it is?

DOCTOR: I'm certain of it! Imagine: she's been lonely for so long - unfulfilled - and then. She finds a man like Laurent. Haven't you seen them together? They can't keep their eyes off each other.

MME RAQUIN: Really, Doctor -

Madame Raquin is too embarrassed to talk further.

DOCTOR: I haven't finished telling you about my girl. Well, to cut a long story short, after a few dead ends, a few wrong turns, I spied her. In a window one day last week as I walked past!

MME RAQUIN: I hope she didn't see you.

DOCTOR: Of course not. But now I know where she lives.

MME RAQUIN: But that's – that's dishonest, Doctor! It's -

DOCTOR: 'When there's no danger in the fight, there's no glory in the triumph.' Corneille

MME RAQUIN: She's probably married.

DOCTOR: She's not. I saw her hanging out the washing: no trousers. Not a male garment to be seen on the line! I'm convinced she lives alone with her mother! They even have a sweet little dog.

MME RAQUIN: (sour) She sounds perfect.

DOCTOR: That's why I've decided to talk to her tomorrow.

MME RAQUIN: And what will you do when she makes it clear your attentions are unwelcome?

DOCTOR: Then so be it. I'll be heartbroken. A confirmed bachelor once more. But no one can say I didn't try just once in my life to find true happiness.

MME RAQUIN: You're being an idiot. Do you know who you remind me of? My brother – off on his wild goose chase half way across Africa. It's not right!

DOCTOR: Well I blame this house. There's love in the air. It must be infectious! If music be the food of love, play on.

Madame Raquin looks utterly bewildered.

23.

Laurent and Thérèse are in the bedroom. Laurent tries to touch her – she rejects him.

LAURENT: Surely we didn't kill Camille just to end up like this.

He moves closer to her. Her skin crawls, but she tries not to push him away. he touches her, puts his arms round her. Suddenly she can't take it.

THÉRÈSE: No, don't –

She pushes him away. He comes back.

THÉRÈSE: This isn't the way.

She tries to push him away, but he holds tight.

THÉRÈSE: Laurent, stop!

Thérèse struggles. Laurent's stronger. He pulls up her skirts.

Suddenly she bites hard into his neck – where Camille bit him. He hurtles away in agony.

LAURENT: Jesus Christ, are you completely insane?

They stare at each other, in agony, hating each other.

LAURENT: Bitch!

Suddenly Camille appears at the door. He howls at them in derision: enjoying their agony. They're startled. But before they can pursue him, he's gone and there's knocking at the same door.

MME RAQUIN: (outside) Thérèse, Laurent?
THÉRÈSE: We're just getting up.
MME RAQUIN: (outside) Are you not coming down for dinner?
LAURENT: Dinner?
MME RAQUIN: (outside) Breakfast is ready.
THÉRÈSE: What time is it?
LAURENT: (calling) We're getting ready for bed.
MME RAQUIN: (outside) It's time to get up.
THÉRÈSE: We slept in.
MME RAQUIN: You can't stay in there all day.
LAURENT: What's the time?
MME RAQUIN: (outside) I'll make you a nice nightcap.
LAURENT: (calling) WHAT TIME IS IT??
THÉRÈSE: It's late, let me sleep!
MME RAQUIN: (calling) Laurent, hurry, you'll be late for work.

Time has gone haywire. Laurent and Thérèse are dressed.

24.
Downstairs, the Doctor and Madame Raquin have prepared the dominoes.

MME RAQUIN: (calling) The Doctor's here, children!
DOCTOR: Oh, they don't want to see an old fool when they have other things in mind. Won't be much longer now, I'd

wager.
MME RAQUIN: What won't be long?
DOCTOR: You'll see, grandmaman!

Madame Raquin understands.

MME RAQUIN: You really think so?
DOCTOR: As inevitable as the earth rotating round the sun. As me finding my girl in blue.
MME RAQUIN: What? No. (Calling, to avoid this conversation) Thérèse! Laurent!
DOCTOR: I spoke to her, Madame Raquin.
MME RAQUIN: And she told you you were mad, I hope? The poor thing must have got quite a fright. Doctor, you must stop this behaviour, it's not befitting someone your age.
DOCTOR: She came for a drink with me.
MME RAQUIN: With a complete stranger – What kind of woman would do such a thing?
DOCTOR: It went – well. As well as could be expected. We talked. She's all on her own with only her mother for company. Actually she's thrilled to have a suitor.
MME RAQUIN: You're a suitor now, are you? After one drink. You're probably her mother's age! Are you sure you're not after the wrong woman?
DOCTOR: Actually it's been more than one drink now.
MME RAQUIN: Then she's after your money.
DOCTOR: So?
MME RAQUIN: You need to be careful. You don't know how the world works –
DOCTOR: She likes me. She finds me hilarious. Madame Raquin, she's enchanting. It's a perfect match.
MME RAQUIN: Nonsense! She's turning you into a perfect fool.

The Doctor is hurt by Madame Raquin's reaction.

DOCTOR: Love makes fools of us all, dear lady. Perhaps I should stop coming here.
MME RAQUIN: No, Doctor -

Before Madame Raquin can say more, Thérèse and Laurent come in.

DOCTOR: How delightful to see you both!
LAURENT: Doctor!
DOCTOR: Looking well, looking very well. Well? Any good news?

Laurent and Thérèse don't respond.

DOCTOR: When's the christening?
THÉRÈSE: (panicked) Sorry?
DOCTOR: Look at you. Like two turtle doves, inseparable for life! So much in love, you barely have time for us mere mortals. Well, it's probably not such bad timing: my life is changing too – I was just telling your mother. I might not be able to visit so much in future.
LAURENT: But that's unthinkable -
DOCTOR: Well, I'm flattered, of course -
LAURENT: How will we spend our evenings?
DOCTOR: Now don't exaggerate, Laurent, you're hardly lacking for company, are you?

Laurent and Thérèse look at each other. The Doctor sees their look.

DOCTOR: See how happy they are! They may not say much, but - love doesn't need words. Isn't it wonderful!

Madame Raquin starts to laugh, almost hysterical. As does the Doctor, happy. Thérèse and Laurent join in the laughter, as they settle down to play dominoes.

LAURENT: Oh, did I tell you I've given up my job?
MME RAQUIN: No!
DOCTOR: But what are you going to live on?
LAURENT: I'm going to rent a small studio. Make a stab at being a painter before I'm too old.
MME RAQUIN: Well, this is a surprise.
LAURENT: It's now or never.
MME RAQUIN: Thérèse, what do you think of this?

Thérèse says nothing. She didn't know.

LAURENT: Can't an artist dream? We have enough money, don't we?
MME RAQUIN: Well, perhaps if we're very careful –
LAURENT: Honestly, my work at the office is sheer drudgery. It leaves me with no energy. Now I'm going to work just as hard. Harder! All the hours God gives me in order to make this thing work, you'll see. There's an opportunity, right now, a studio with a friend.

He sees their look.

LAURENT: I thought you'd support me.
MME RAQUIN: Of course we do, Laurent. If that's what you really want. I'm just surprised, now you have responsibilities –
LAURENT: Of course I can make money if that's all you want. But I want to – to do more with my life. Really find out what I'm made of –

DOCTOR: Well, we only live once.
MME RAQUIN: Thérèse?

Thérèse is silent.

MME RAQUIN: Thérèse, why don't you say something?

Thérèse still doesn't answer.

25.
Thérèse and Laurent fight around the silent, unmoving figures of the Doctor and Madame Raquin.

THÉRÈSE: You're just doing this because you can't get your hands on her money!
LAURENT: For God's sake, don't you understand, I want to paint!
THÉRÈSE: No, you want to go back to your old life. You want to escape me! Well, I won't let you fritter away what little we have!
LAURENT: Just try and stop me.

Laurent is determined. Thérèse is furious.

THÉRÈSE: If you leave the office you'll no longer have an income, you realise that? You'll have to depend entirely on me, is that what you really want?

Laurent shrugs.

THÉRÈSE: My Aunt left the capital to me, not you!

Laurent looks at her oddly.

THÉRÈSE: Don't you threaten me –
LAURENT: Did I say anything? Your stupid bitch of an aunt's on my side. She thinks I'm the new Camille.
THÉRÈSE: You won't blackmail me!
LAURENT: I get a hundred francs a month to cover my expenses out of the two thousand francs a month investment income.
THÉRÈSE: You've got this all worked out, haven't you?
LAURENT: The shop income covers the rents on the shop and my studio –
THÉRÈSE: Don't do this -
LAURENT: The capital remains untouched.

Thérèse is stopped in her tracks. He really has worked it all out.

THÉRÈSE: Untouched? Until when?
LAURENT: I don't need it.
THÉRÈSE: Until when??

But Laurent is implacable.

THÉRÈSE: Never go over your allowance. Promise me!

Laurent says nothing.

THÉRÈSE: You'll never get your hands on the capital without my signature. And I'll never sign.

Camille watches from the distance. Thérèse leaves, isolating Laurent.

26.

The studio forms round Laurent – he's painting. The studio's five by three metres with one large window, shedding a harsh, white light on the floor and walls: it's like a burial vault made of grey clay.

Laurent paints like a man possessed.

There's a knock on the door. He ignores it. The knocking continues.

LAURENT: (calling) I've told you, the rent will be paid!

More knocking.

LAURENT: (calling) For Christ's sake, so I'm a bit short at the moment, so?!

Finally Laurent hurls down his paintbrush and heads for the door.

But it's not the landlady. It's the Doctor.

DOCTOR: I hope I'm not disturbing you. I er… happened to be passing.
LAURENT: Doctor?
DOCTOR: A friend lives near-by.
LAURENT: Thérèse sent you.
DOCTOR: No, no. To be honest, I half expected to find her here too. I know it can be difficult sometimes. Privacy for the young.
LAURENT: I have to get back to my work.
DOCTOR: May I see?
LAURENT: No!
DOCTOR: Ah. The great artist at work.

LAURENT: How did you find me?

DOCTOR: Madame Raquin. She wants to know you have everything you need.

LAURENT: (not believing him) Well tell her she's nothing to fear. Look, no models, nothing but my work.

DOCTOR: She worries about you. Giving up your job so suddenly. Laurent, if it's something I've done. If I come round too much.

LAURENT: Jesus, you think this is about you?

Now the Doctor sees the pictures for the first time.

DOCTOR: My God, did you do these?

LAURENT: Oh, they're just sketches.

DOCTOR: No, really, who did them?

LAURENT: What are you talking about, man?

The penny drops.

DOCTOR: But they're wonderful. Truly…extraordinary. So you have been working! To be honest, I thought – Madame Raquin and I – we both - I didn't realise. You're a serious artist.

Laurent says nothing.

DOCTOR: Madame Raquin will be pleased. Delighted! But. But a word of advice – I've only one little criticism, if criticism you can call it with work such as this. Your – your studies have a certain physical - similarity. You're painting the same face. My God, even the women.

Then the Doctor realises.

DOCTOR: Oh my God.
LAURENT: What?
DOCTOR: The face –
LAURENT: What?
DOCTOR: My God, poor you!

The Doctor is looking at Laurent in a strange way.

LAURENT: What? Doctor, what is it?
DOCTOR: Tell me you've realised too.
LAURENT: Doctor, don't.
DOCTOR: It's Camille.
LAURENT: No!
DOCTOR: They're all Camille. Look for yourself.

The Doctor looks at Laurent in an entirely different way now. Laurent's shocked.

DOCTOR: Well, I must be on my way. I shall tell Madame Raquin you're - well. No reason to worry her, is there? Well, keep up the good work. Only – this is my advice as a Doctor. Only - paint someone else. This - can't be doing you - or your marriage - any good – no good at all.

The Doctor hurriedly leaves, Laurent's left with the pictures. He breathes heavily.

Something moves in the shadows. Or someone.

LAURENT: (to Camille) Just leave me alone!!

Hurriedly Laurent starts to draw again – thick broad strokes with charcoal. But Camille appears on the canvas.

Whenever Laurent paints, Camille appears. Laurent stares at his hand in horror. Then tries to destroy the paintings. Like a madman possessed. As he attacks, light crashes round him, splits around him.

CAMILLE: Magnificent.

Laurent swings round, startled. The overhead light suddenly swings wildly. But he can't see Camille.

27.
The Doctor talks to Madame Raquin and Thérèse at a distance, at their home:

DOCTOR: Magnificent! You have nothing to worry about. He is truly gifted. Such a depth of suffering -

The Doctor doesn't see that Madame Raquin isn't really listening. She looks glazed.

DOCTOR: Of course, I killed two birds with one stone. You know my little bird in blue, yes? She's agreed to marry me! Yes, actually agreed to be mine!
MME RAQUIN: Oh -

There's a loud scream. It could be the cats, it could be another murder with the glinting knife. It's also Laurent smashing up the last of paintings. Simultaneously Camille throws a dustbin and lid against the wall/floor: rotten rubbish goes everywhere. And Madame Raquin slumps over, with a groan.

Thérèse rushes to her Aunt.

THÉRÈSE: Aunt –
DOCTOR: Madame Raquin, can you hear me?
THÉRÈSE: Aunt, the Doctor's here. Try to speak, tell us what happened.

All that comes out of Madame Raquin are rasping noises. She's had a stroke. The Doctor looks into Madame Raquin's eyes: they don't respond to light.

DOCTOR: Make a sign.

Laurent arrives while this is going on.

DOCTOR: Your Aunt's had a seizure. She'll need to be watched all the time. (to Laurent, about Thérèse) Look after her. I'm sorry, Thérèse. Truly. I know how upsetting this must be.

Madame Raquin dribbles. Her feet and hands are cold. She can mumble, but barely move. Madame Raquin looks as if she's trying to say something with her eyes.

DOCTOR: Don't worry – you have Thérèse and Laurent to look after you now. Love surrounding you. You'll be right as rain in no time, I'm quite sure of it.

The Doctor takes Thérèse to one side.

DOCTOR: She won't ever be herself again. But she won't die. She could live to be a hundred.
THÉRÈSE: Oh no –
DOCTOR: I know you're upset. I'm sorry. But you can help her. You understand what she's saying.

Madame Raquin tries to speak. The Doctor interprets.

DOCTOR: 'If this is what God wills, I'm happy.' Yes, Madame Raquin, that's right. God is with you, dear lady.

Madame Raquin is saying anything but this.

DOCTOR: You're lucky. You're in the very best hands.

The Doctor leaves.

Laurent and Thérèse are trapped.

28.
The clock ticks. Thérèse and Laurent sit opposite each other. Laurent lowers the lampshade to avoid having to look at Thérèse.

Madame Raquin sits between them, her face a decayed death mask with two living eyes in the middle. She starts to fall asleep.

LAURENT: Madame Raquin?

Madame Raquin wakes, mumbles.

LAURENT: You don't want to sleep, do you?
THÉRÈSE: No, look, she's happy staying up with us, aren't you?

Silence, Madame Raquin smiling benignly on them.

THÉRÈSE: (to Madame Raquin) Do you want anything? A game of dominoes?

LAURENT: Does she look like can play dominoes?

Madame Raquin falls back to sleep.

LAURENT: I have to get out of here –
THÉRÈSE: Where to?
LAURENT: The studio –
THÉRÈSE: I thought you'd given up.
LAURENT: For a drink then!
THÉRÈSE: Laurent, she's awake!
LAURENT: Because you woke her!
THÉRÈSE: Laurent, please, stay -
LAURENT: Why? You can't stand being near me!
THÉRÈSE: She's a human being -
LAURENT: You never had such qualms about her son!
THÉRÈSE: Shh - !
LAURENT: Before I met you I was innocent!
THÉRÈSE: Laurent, NO!

Camille appears behind his mother.

LAURENT: (seeing Camille) Get away from me! She forced me to drown you, it was nothing to do with me!
THÉRÈSE: Stop this now!

Thérèse slaps Laurent. Laurent is about to hit Thérèse back but she flees to the other side of Madame Raquin.

Too late - Madame Raquin has opened her eyes, seems to understand. Despair falls over her. Camille has disappeared. A great tear rolls down Madame Raquin's face, a wordless, heart-rending grief.

THÉRÈSE: Look what you've done now! (suddenly feeling

pity) We must put her to bed.

Laurent looks at her, is about to help Madame Raquin, but sees the aunt's look.

LAURENT: That's right, take a good look. You can't touch me, you stupid old cow...

He heads off to bed.

THÉRÈSE: Laurent, please, she needs to go to bed –
LAURENT: Do it yourself.

Laurent is about to leave the room, when Camille suddenly appears. He seems to smack Laurent in the head – without touching him - pushing him back.

Simultaneously papers shoot into the room: torn paintings and drawings, all of Camille.

The room gets smaller - it is now a complete mess and a living prison.

29.
Laurent is increasingly hit by savage headaches: Camille continues to push Laurent's head - without touching him - as if he is controlling him. Thérèse tries to help, while Madame Raquin sits immobile, watching.

LAURENT: Uh –
THÉRÈSE: Laurent –
LAURENT: I can't see –
THÉRÈSE: Drink some water, at least.
LAURENT: I don't need water.

THÉRÈSE: Something must help –
LAURENT: Don't touch me!

Thérèse doesn't know what to do.

LAURENT: She's no better. Sitting there, watching. What is it with you, woman?
THÉRÈSE: What do you want me to do – turn her face to the wall?
LAURENT: Her eyes follow me!
THÉRÈSE: You're imagining it. Please -
LAURENT: Plotting revenge –
THÉRÈSE: Talk sense, how can she?
LAURENT: And you! Look at this place! It's a mess!
THÉRÈSE: And what about you? Take a look at yourself!

As he says this there's a knock on the door.

THÉRÈSE: Who is it?

Thérèse tries to smarten herself up. Laurent doesn't bother. The Doctor pops his head in. He's shocked at the state of the place. Camille circles, predatory, unseen.

DOCTOR: Mind if I - ? Ah, Laurent, not busy? Any luck with the painting? Thérèse, now there's a face to paint, a Madonna! And how's the old lady? How are we today? Feeling better, I hope, Madame Raquin?

The Doctor treats Madame Raquin a bit like a small child, raises his voice as if she's deaf.

DOCTOR: Sorry, bit busy, yes. You'll never believe it – I got married! To the most wonderful girl in the world. I wanted you there, but – you know how it is. A quiet, family ceremony was just what the Doctor ordered. (he laughs heartily) Just her mother, and siblings, really. Some of her brothers were a bit odd, but what of it? Twenty six years my junior, but I couldn't be happier. She's given me the night off! Probably wants to meet a lover. I'm joking! But what if it were true? The heart doesn't mind what the eye doesn't see.

Madame Raquin tries to talk.

DOCTOR: What's that? Thérèse and Laurent? What are you trying to say, Madame Raquin?

He tries to read the answer in her eyes. Thérèse and Laurent watch like hawks.

DOCTOR: Looking after you very well, are they? Good, good.

Madame Raquin throws a ferocious look.

DOCTOR: You want to move? Wonderful, that's excellent, dear lady. They'll be able to help you.

A huge effort now from Madame Raquin – meanwhile Camille starts to writes something in blood red across the back wall. Madame Raquin slurs badly.

MME RAQUIN: Lsn –
DOCTOR: 'Listen'! Yes?
MME RAQUIN: Tese and Lren –
DOCTOR: Thérèse and Laurent, yes?
MME RAQUIN: Mrdrs –

The Doctor struggles a bit harder with this word, even as Camille finishes writing the word 'Murderers' across the back wall..

DOCTOR: Mothers? Marvellous, yes! You're been a good mother to them, and now they're going to be good children. I'm sorry, I must go. Can't keep my wonderful bride waiting.
MME RAQUIN: Plse -
DOCTOR: Pillows! Plenty of pillows, you two. Keep her comfortable at all times. Well, au revoir.

The Doctor heads out. Thérèse and Laurent's relief is immense.

Thérèse suddenly feels nauseous. And faint. She feels her stomach.

30.
Laurent and Thérèse argue in the dining room – a damp, vault-like room lit only by the yellowish glow of the lamp.

Madame Raquin watches them, half in and out of sleep.

LAURENT: You think I like this any better than she does?

Thérèse is crying.

LAURENT: Now what are you crying for? For God's sake -
THÉRÈSE: You know why…
LAURENT: Well, you shouldn't have killed him, should you?

THÉRÈSE: It wasn't me!

LAURENT: Jesus! Alright, pretend you've forgotten. Allow me to refresh your memory.

THÉRÈSE: Laurent, no!

LAURENT: You were by the edge of the river, remember? I whispered 'I'm going to push him in' -

THÉRÈSE: That's not what happened!

LAURENT: And you agreed! Got into the boat with me –

THÉRÈSE: It's not true, I wasn't thinking straight, I don't remember –

Madame Raquin's eyes have flicked open.

LAURENT: Don't believe a word she says, she tricked me!

THÉRÈSE: I never wanted him dead!

LAURENT: I was an honest man living an honest life before I met you!

THÉRÈSE: It's my evidence against yours.

Laurent stops.

LAURENT: You really think you can threaten me?

An impasse: Laurent and Thérèse know they're both guilty. Madame Raquin's fixed stare never leaves them.

Thérèse falls at Madame Raquin's feet.

THÉRÈSE: Please, forgive me! She does! Look, she forgives me!

Thérèse kisses Madame Raquin – who would dearly like to pull away, but can't.

LAURENT: Stop this, it's disgusting!

Laurent drags Thérèse to her feet.

THÉRÈSE: Laurent, we're both guilty, we must confess -
LAURENT: Stop torturing the poor woman, can't you see what you're doing to her!

Madame Raquin continues staring. Thérèse fusses over her, straightens her pillow.

THÉRÈSE: Oh maman, he was such a good man.
LAURENT: He was stupid. He got on your nerves, the man smelt of carbolic soap and cabbage!
THÉRÈSE: Bravo! You know nothing about a woman's heart, do you? How kind he was. Camille loved me, and I loved him.
LAURENT: Oh, really? Then tell me why his doughy flesh made you sick?
THÉRÈSE: I loved him as a sister! He was noble -
LAURENT: Jesus, you couldn't make it up, could you? The loyal little widow -
THÉRÈSE: And we killed him, God, we killed him. Oh God, oh God, oh God -
LAURENT: Shut up!

Laurent paces up and down.

THÉRÈSE: I'm sorry. It's my fault he killed Camille -
LAURENT: SILENCE, WOMAN!

Laurent is now drunk with rage. He throws himself upon her, knocks her to the ground, and holds her down with his knee. He raises his fist.

THÉRÈSE: That's right, do what you do best…murderer! Camille never once lifted a finger to me!

Laurent proceeds to beat her up. Camille watches from the shadows.

Thérèse leaves, slowly.

Laurent scratches his neck obsessively. He has to undo his collar. His neck's livid red. He turns to Madame Raquin.

LAURENT: Just stop looking at me!

Laurent follows Thérèse out.

31.
Camille is left with Madame Raquin. She senses something, knows he's there, but not where. Madame Raquin tries to talk.

CAMILLE: Don't worry, maman. Not long now.

Camille wipes her dribbling mouth, caresses her. Gives her something to drink. She drinks thirstily as if she hasn't had water for a long time.

CAMILLE: (sings) Sur le pont d'Avignon
On y danse on y danse
Sur le pont d'Avignon
On y danse tout en rond

A lullaby. A harmony with the full cast. A moment of beauty. Peace.

32.

A bruised Thérèse returns with a crash, she's drunk. Madame Raquin and Camille sit in the half light, his head in her lap. Laurent follows Thérèse in. She drops something.

LAURENT: Where've you been?
THÉRÈSE: I'm going to bed.

Thérèse starts to head off.

LAURENT: I want five thousand francs.
THÉRÈSE: No.
LAURENT: Did I give you a choice?
THÉRÈSE: Right, you chuck in your job, business has fallen apart, we can barely live on the interest from the dowry! Every day I have to break into our capital just to feed you. That's all you ever wanted: food and drink!

Laurent goes pale. Then, unsteadily, he says:

LAURENT: Listen, there's no point arguing, for either of us. The sensible thing would be to come to an understanding.
THÉRÈSE: Meaning?
LAURENT: If we don't want something dreadful to happen. I asked for five thousand francs because that's what I need.
THÉRÈSE: And I've already told you -

Laurent rises abruptly to his feet. Thérèse is afraid he is about to hit her. She hunches into a ball. But Laurent doesn't even go near her.

LAURENT: Fine, I'll talk to the police.

THÉRÈSE: You? Brave enough? No, I'll go.

Thérèse heads for the stairs. She's already outside, when Laurent loses his nerve.

LAURENT: Thérèse, no!

Thérèse comes back.

THÉRÈSE: You're right. It's stupid to quarrel over money. Sooner or later you'll waste it all anyway. Here, have it! Take it, take it all, it's all yours!

Thérèse gets out a stash of money and throws it at Laurent. He grabs what he can and flees.

33.
Thérèse can't sit still. She's aware of Camille's presence. Claustrophobia: dripping pipes; steam coming out of the sewers/streets – mist; the never ending black wall. She tries to pray.

Camille talks to his unmoving mother.

CAMILLE: Do you remember the river at Vernon? You remember my friend Laurent, you gave him shoes for school because he only had farmer's boots? You always said how well he'd do, he was so fearless.

He shakes. He is disintegrating.

CAMILLE: I can't see my hand. What's happened to my hand, maman? I can see right through.

Suddenly Thérèse is holding a knife.

The Doctor's there. Thérèse hides the knife.

DOCTOR: She's the same, I'm afraid. We must pray that God will be merciful.
THÉRÈSE: She looks worse.
DOCTOR: There's no change, Thérèse, I can assure you. But she tells me she's happy. With you two. Are you sure your face is all right?
THÉRÈSE: I fell. Against the door.

The Doctor lingers

THÉRÈSE: You don't believe me?
DOCTOR: No, it's - Thérèse, I'm sorry, it's a final goodbye.
THÉRÈSE: Au revoir.
DOCTOR: We're moving. Out of Paris. My wife's expecting a child. And – the city's… too dirty for us. Too dangerous. Another woman was killed last week. A girl. Fourteen. Abigail. She lived two doors down from us. It makes you think.
THÉRÈSE: But you're her friend. You can't leave her!

The Doctor looks awkward.

DOCTOR: I have to move on. She has you two…
THÉRÈSE: You're deserting us!
DOCTOR: If it's too much, you could get a maid -
THÉRÈSE: What with?
DOCTOR: Your capital. Madame Raquin was always careful with her money.
THÉRÈSE: You don't understand, you'll never understand!

You never understood one thing!
DOCTOR: I can see you're upset, it's distressing when something like this happens. But I must do what's right for my own family.
THÉRÈSE: (hard) You tell her. She's all yours.
DOCTOR: No. No, I think better not.

The Doctor is really upset now. It has been a long haul.

DOCTOR I really don't think I can. I'm sorry. I'm so very very sorry.
THÉRÈSE: You can see yourself out.
DOCTOR: Thérèse, I assure you, if there was any other way -
THÉRÈSE: Just go!

He's still lingering.

DOCTOR: Er...Thérèse. Something was removed from my bag yesterday, yes? When I was here. Something important. I really must – must insist it's returned.
THÉRÈSE: Christ, get out, go on, get out, can't you take a hint, you stupid, horrible little self-serving man –
DOCTOR: Thérèse, please –
THÉRÈSE: GET OUT, GET OUT, GO, DOCTOR, GO!

The Doctor finally leaves.

Laurent appears at the door.

THÉRÈSE: Where were you?
LAURENT: Out.
THÉRÈSE: Who with?
LAURENT: No one. How is she?

THÉRÈSE: What do you care?

Thérèse holds out her hands. Laurent sees the knife.

LAURENT: It's funny. I stole poison from the Doctor for the same reason.

A moment of understanding.

LAURENT: Thérèse, we loved each other.
THÉRÈSE: Did we?
LAURENT: Loved each other so much we would have done anything. The light in your eyes. The way you looked at me.

But Camille is there too.

CAMILLE: The cruel eyes of a murderer -
THÉRÈSE: No! I don't remember.
LAURENT: (trying again) We dreamed of each other.
CAMILLE: Hated each other -
LAURENT: Breathed each other -
CAMILLE: Suffocated -
LAURENT: Became each other -
CAMILLE: Drowned -
THÉRÈSE: Laurent, no!
LAURENT: You do remember, don't you? You can't not remember!!
THÉRÈSE/CAMILLE: Better not to remember -
LAURENT: If I say I loved you – still love you. He's dead, Thérèse. We can make him go away for good.
THÉRÈSE: We can't kill a dead man.
CAMILLE: You married a woman who was married to a drowned man -
LAURENT: We can destroy him.

THÉRÈSE: No we can't.
LAURENT: DON'T TELL ME THIS WAS ALL FOR NOTHING - I COULDN'T BEAR IT IF IT ALL MEANT NOTHING!!

Both of them are stopped by this. Silence.

LAURENT: We could have children –
THÉRÈSE: A family, yes!
LAURENT: Thérèse, we could have done anything.
THÉRÈSE: Oh, Laurent. Hold me - Hold me, oh hold me, oh hold me, oh hold me –

She holds out her arms as she did on the boat. Rain starts to fall. The walls close in.

They begin to cry, almost with relief. Suddenly Laurent moves towards her –

LAURENT: Love me –

Already there is knocking at the door.

THÉRÈSE: I love you –
LAURENT: Always love me, Thérèse – now you are mine – you would do anything for me.
DOCTOR: (off) Thérèse, Laurent?
THÉRÈSE: I am yours. I belong to you, I breathe for you, do what you want with me, take what you want, you have me…
DOCTOR: (off) The police are on their way, yes? I had to call them, I'm so sorry. I really do need my medicine back.
THÉRÈSE: Yes.

Laurent drinks the poison, then kisses Thérèse passionately. He dies in her arms. She collapses to the floor with him, groggy, his head in her lap.

Thumping at the door now:

DOCTOR: (off) Now come on, Laurent, open up – don't be stupid -

The bottle drops to the floor. Madame Raquin watches, a faint smile.

Finally the Doctor bursts in, an umbrella over his head – it's pouring outside.

Shadows. The chorus of death hovering. The sound of the room, the city, the world flooding with water.

The Doctor is lost.

DOCTOR: Thérèse - ?

Thérèse starts scrabbling to get the poison.

DOCTOR: Oh God, Thérèse, what have you done?

Thérèse gets the poison, drinks, just before the Doctor realises what is happening.

DOCTOR: Thérèse, no!

The Doctor grabs it, too late. Thérèse holds upright a moment, proud, transcendent – then collapses into Laurent's arms.

All the walls are gone. It's raining. The chorus watch.

Camille watches his mother. Madame Raquin sits, the smile growing on her lips. Camille begins to leave through the water. And we hear 'Sur le Pont d'Avignon' and children's voices, the distant clatter of sabots on cobbles, feet splashing in the rain. Life goes on....

The chorus gradually fade into the darkness, through the water. And finally Camille too washed clean, is gone.

Only Laurent and Thérèse are left, dead in each other's arms.

Gradual fade to darkness.

ENDS.

ALSO BY JEREMY RAISON

THE RAIN GATHERING
Two actors (1m, 1f)

A twenty something couple meet at the end of their relationship. The story of their doomed love affair is revealed in flashbacks. This award-winning play was a big hit at the National Theatre, the Traverse Theatre and on Radio 4.

WAKE ME IN THE MORNING
Three actors (2m, 1f)

The most famous actress in the world. The most powerful man. A brutal battle of the sexes leads to tragedy. Shades of Monroe and Kennedy in this acclaimed stage play premiered in Glasgow at Oran Mor's A Play, A Pie and a Pint.

BRING ME SUNSHINE
Four actors (2m, 2f)

Eric isn't feeling well. He feels worse when he realises Ernie is doing his funeral oration. Carol wants her husband back. Angie needs to help. A moving comedy featuring two men who may or may not be Eric Morecambe and Ernie Wise.

CANDYLAND
Three actors (2m, 1f)

Star has retreated to an aircraft hangar in the middle of the Nevada desert to live in peaceful seclusion with the woman he loves. Then City turns up uninvited. Soon it becomes clear that Star's idyllic isolation is not all it seems.

THE SOUND OF MY VOICE
Two actors (1m, 1f)

Morris Magellan is a successful executive, but he is also a chronic alcoholic. This Ron Butlin adaptation was a great success for the Citizens Theatre, receiving 4 awards and seven 5 star reviews.

HEART AND SOUL
Seven Actors (4m, 3f)

Old school-friends reform their band for a wedding. They're twenty years older and have grown apart. Then the last member of the band appears - the only one to have had huge success in her musical career - and sparks fly.

www.ingramcontent.com/pod-product-compliance
Lightning Source LLC
LaVergne TN
LVHW051646080426
835511LV00016B/2528